Pre-Algebra

Table of Contents

Fractions
Simplifying Fractions 4
Adding and Subtracting Fractions
  with Like Denominators 6
Adding and Subtracting Fractions
  with Unlike Denominators 7
Adding and Subtracting Mixed Numbers 9
Adding and Subtracting Mixed Numbers Practice 10
Multiplying Fractions 11
Dividing Fractions 13
Mixed Practice with Fractions 15
Problem Solving with Fractions 16

Decimals
Writing Fractions as Decimals 17
Rounding Decimals 19
Multiplying and Dividing by Powers of 10 20
Adding Decimals 21
Subtracting Decimals 23
Multiplying Decimals 25
Multiplying Decimals Using a Calculator 26
Dividing Decimals 27
Dividing Decimals Using a Calculator 28
Mixed Practice with Decimals 29
Problem Solving with Decimals 31
Writing Decimals as Fractions 32

Ratios, Proportions, and Percents
Ratios 34
Proportions 36
Problem Solving with Proportions 37
Percents 38
Problem Solving with Percents 41

Integers
Adding Integers with Like Signs 42
Adding Integers with Unlike Signs 44
Subtracting Integers 46
Adding and Subtracting Integers 48
Multiplying Integers 49
Dividing Integers 51
Mixed Practice with Integers 53
Problem Solving with Integers 54

Real Numbers
Adding and Subtracting Real Numbers 55
Multiplying and Dividing Real Numbers 57
Order of Operations with Real Numbers 59
Comparing Real Numbers 61

Equations
Open Sentences 62
Evaluating Expressions 64
Simplifying Expressions 65
Solving Addition Equations 69
Solving Subtraction Equations 70
Solving Addition and Subtraction Equations 71
Solving Multiplication Equations 72
Solving Division Equations 74
Solving Multiplication and Division Equations 75
Solving Equations with Two Operations 76
Solving Equations Using the Distributive Property ... 77
Solving Equations 78
Mixed Practice with Equations 79

Problem Solving
Writing Algebraic Expressions 80

Inequalities
Number Lines.. 87
Solving Inequalities with Addition
  and Subtraction 88
Solving Inequalities with Multiplication
  and Division 89
Solving Inequalities... 90
Solving Inequalities with Multiple Operations 94
Solving Inequalities with Variables on Both Sides 95
Practice Solving Inequalities 96

Ordered Pairs and Graphing
Plotting Points 98
Graphing Linear Equations..................................... 100

Answer Key 104

Kelley Wingate
An imprint of Carson-Dellosa Publishing LLC
PO Box 35665 • Greensboro, NC 27425 USA

ISBN 978-1-60418-265-1

How to Use This Book

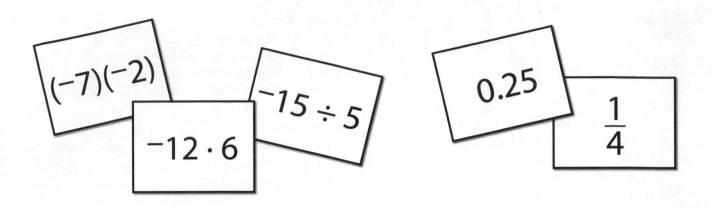

This book was designed to help students practice and master mathematics skills. The stronger their foundation is, the easier it will be for them to move into higher levels of mathematics.

The activities in this book cover such topics as fractions, decimals, integers, real numbers, equations, and basic graphing. The pages may be used as supplemental material, or as enrichment for any pre-algebra program. After completing the pages in this book, students will be adequately prepared for the study of algebra.

All students learn at their own rate; therefore, use your judgment to introduce concepts when it is developmentally appropriate.

Hands-On Learning

Hands-on learning reinforces the skills covered within the activity pages and improves students' potential for understanding. The flash cards at the back of this book may be utilized for basic skill and enrichment activities. Pull the flash cards out and cut them apart. Use the flash cards as practice and reinforcement of basic algebraic concepts.

How to Use This Book

Resources

Writing Fractions as Decimals

If you are changing a fraction to a decimal, you should divide. For example, to change the fraction $\frac{1}{2}$ to a decimal, you would divide 1 by 2.

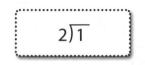

Writing Decimals as Fractions

When changing a decimal to a fraction, look at the number of places after the decimal point. That number is the same as the number of zeros in the denominator. For example, the decimal 0.08 has two places after the decimal point, so the fraction will be $\frac{8}{100}$.

Order of Operations

When performing problems that include order of operations, you should make a priority pyramid. This will serve as a useful tool.

Order of Operations Pyramid

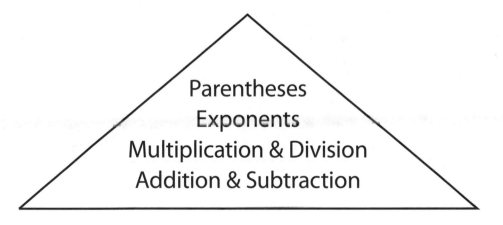

Parentheses
Exponents
Multiplication & Division
Addition & Subtraction

Fractions

Simplifying Fractions

$$\frac{3}{6} \div \frac{3}{3} \text{ (greatest common factor)} = \frac{1}{2}$$

Simplify each fraction by dividing by the greatest common factor.

1. $\frac{5}{15}$

2. $\frac{8}{24}$

3. $\frac{10}{70}$

4. $\frac{13}{39}$

5. $\frac{19}{57}$

6. $\frac{54}{63}$

7. $\frac{6}{39}$

8. $\frac{6}{15}$

9. $\frac{7}{42}$

10. $\frac{35}{35}$

11. $\frac{9}{36}$

12. $\frac{45}{72}$

13. $\frac{32}{136}$

14. $\frac{6}{48}$

15. $\frac{30}{45}$

16. $\frac{27}{81}$

17. $\frac{56}{74}$

18. $\frac{16}{72}$

19. $\frac{56}{63}$

20. $\frac{7}{70}$

21. $\frac{12}{18}$

Fractions

Simplifying Fractions

$$\frac{18}{14} \div \frac{2}{2} = \frac{9}{7}$$

Improper Fraction

$$\frac{18}{14} \div \frac{2}{2} = \frac{9}{7} = \frac{7}{7} + \frac{2}{7} = 1 + \frac{2}{7} = 1\frac{2}{7}$$

Mixed Number

Simplify each improper fraction. Then, write each reduced improper fraction as a mixed number.

1. $\frac{15}{9}$

2. $\frac{36}{24}$

3. $\frac{28}{20}$

4. $\frac{66}{19}$

5. $\frac{45}{27}$

6. $\frac{27}{21}$

7. $\frac{45}{36}$

8. $\frac{69}{18}$

9. $\frac{22}{8}$

10. $\frac{36}{10}$

11. $\frac{20}{12}$

12. $\frac{27}{24}$

13. $\frac{50}{30}$

14. $\frac{30}{12}$

Fractions

Adding and Subtracting Fractions with Like Denominators

$$\frac{1}{8} + \frac{3}{8} = \frac{4}{8} = \frac{1}{2} \qquad \frac{5}{8} - \frac{1}{8} = \frac{4}{8} = \frac{1}{2}$$

Add or subtract. Write the answer in simplest form.

1. $\frac{4}{15} - \frac{1}{15} =$ **2.** $\frac{11}{12} + \frac{9}{12} =$ **3.** $\frac{19}{20} - \frac{17}{20} =$

4. $\frac{17}{18} - \frac{8}{18} =$ **5.** $\frac{13}{30} + \frac{11}{30} =$ **6.** $\frac{32}{35} - \frac{17}{35} =$

7. $\frac{13}{24} + \frac{17}{24} =$ **8.** $\frac{3}{21} + \frac{11}{21} =$ **9.** $\frac{16}{18} + \frac{17}{18} =$

10. $\frac{11}{14} - \frac{6}{14} =$ **11.** $\frac{31}{32} + \frac{29}{32} =$ **12.** $\frac{19}{20} - \frac{9}{20} =$

13. $\frac{2}{9} + \frac{3}{9} =$ **14.** $\frac{6}{8} + \frac{7}{8} =$ **15.** $\frac{19}{24} + \frac{23}{24} =$

16. $\frac{23}{25} - \frac{8}{25} =$ **17.** $\frac{13}{15} - \frac{11}{15} =$ **18.** $\frac{16}{17} - \frac{9}{17} =$

Fractions

Adding and Subtracting Fractions with Unlike Denominators

$$\frac{3}{7} + \frac{2}{6} = \frac{18}{42} + \frac{14}{42} = \frac{32}{42} = \frac{16}{21} \qquad \frac{3}{7} - \frac{2}{6} = \frac{18}{42} - \frac{14}{42} = \frac{4}{42} = \frac{2}{21}$$

Solve each problem. Write the answer in simplest form.

1. $\frac{6}{7} + \frac{1}{5} =$

2. $\frac{4}{9} - \frac{1}{3} =$

3. $\frac{3}{4} + \frac{2}{9} =$

4. $\frac{5}{6} + \frac{7}{8} =$

5. $\frac{1}{6} + \frac{7}{9} =$

6. $\frac{9}{25} - \frac{3}{10} =$

7. $\frac{2}{3} - \frac{5}{8} =$

8. $\frac{5}{8} + \frac{11}{12} =$

9. $\frac{2}{5} - \frac{3}{8} =$

10. $\frac{1}{6} + \frac{3}{4} =$

11. $\frac{9}{10} - \frac{7}{20} =$

12. $\frac{5}{10} + \frac{6}{8} =$

13. $\frac{8}{9} - \frac{5}{12} =$

14. $\frac{2}{3} - \frac{2}{5} =$

15. $\frac{1}{4} + \frac{4}{8} =$

16. $\frac{4}{9} + \frac{7}{8} =$

17. $\frac{2}{4} + \frac{3}{7} =$

18. $\frac{7}{10} - \frac{3}{8} =$

Fractions

Adding and Subtracting Fractions with Unlike Denominators

$$\frac{4}{6} + \frac{3}{5} = \frac{20}{30} + \frac{18}{30} = \frac{38}{30} = 1\frac{4}{15} \qquad \frac{4}{6} - \frac{3}{5} = \frac{20}{30} - \frac{18}{30} = \frac{2}{30} = \frac{1}{15}$$

Solve each problem. Write the answer in simplest form.

1. $\frac{2}{6} + \frac{3}{9} =$

2. $\frac{11}{12} - \frac{5}{18} =$

3. $\frac{8}{12} + \frac{7}{8} =$

4. $\frac{17}{21} - \frac{4}{6} =$

5. $\frac{3}{10} + \frac{7}{15} =$

6. $\frac{11}{12} - \frac{3}{6} =$

7. $\frac{7}{15} + \frac{3}{6} =$

8. $\frac{5}{6} - \frac{3}{9} =$

9. $\frac{6}{7} - \frac{3}{5} =$

10. $\frac{11}{15} + \frac{1}{6} =$

11. $\frac{5}{8} + \frac{2}{7} =$

12. $\frac{29}{32} + \frac{7}{8} =$

13. $\frac{4}{5} + \frac{11}{15} =$

14. $\frac{5}{15} - \frac{3}{10} =$

15. $\frac{11}{14} - \frac{1}{6} =$

16. $\frac{8}{9} + \frac{4}{5} =$

17. $\frac{7}{8} + \frac{8}{9} =$

18. $\frac{11}{12} - \frac{5}{15} =$

Fractions

Adding and Subtracting Mixed Numbers

$$3\frac{1}{2} + 1\frac{3}{8} = 3\frac{4}{8} + 1\frac{3}{8} = 4\frac{7}{8}$$

Solve each problem. Write the answer in simplest form.

1. $4\frac{5}{7} - 2\frac{2}{3} =$

2. $9\frac{3}{5} + 4\frac{2}{3} =$

3. $7\frac{1}{2} - 2\frac{7}{10} =$

4. $17\frac{3}{4} - 8\frac{2}{5} =$

5. $16\frac{1}{4} - 7\frac{5}{8} =$

6. $6\frac{2}{7} - 1\frac{1}{3} =$

7. $3\frac{7}{12} + 7\frac{5}{6} =$

8. $4\frac{1}{8} - 3\frac{1}{2} =$

9. $8\frac{1}{8} + 5\frac{3}{4} =$

10. $12\frac{7}{9} + 3\frac{2}{3} =$

11. $4\frac{1}{7} - 3\frac{1}{5} =$

12. $6\frac{4}{5} + 2\frac{3}{9} =$

13. $1\frac{9}{12} - 1\frac{3}{4} =$

14. $4\frac{8}{9} + 2\frac{5}{6} =$

15. $4\frac{3}{6} + 7\frac{3}{8} =$

16. $5\frac{1}{2} - 2\frac{2}{7} =$

17. $2\frac{8}{10} - 1\frac{5}{15} =$

18. $11\frac{4}{5} - 3\frac{5}{6} =$

Fractions

Adding and Subtracting Mixed Numbers Practice

$$2\frac{2}{3} + 6\frac{4}{5} = 2\frac{10}{15} + 6\frac{12}{15} = 8\frac{22}{15} = 9\frac{7}{15}$$

Solve each problem. Write the answer in simplest form.

1. $6\frac{2}{3} - 5\frac{3}{9} =$

2. $6\frac{8}{12} - 5\frac{1}{3} =$

3. $5\frac{5}{9} + 3\frac{4}{6} =$

4. $9\frac{5}{9} - 6\frac{1}{2} =$

5. $14\frac{3}{4} - 8\frac{5}{6} =$

6. $5\frac{2}{9} + 3\frac{3}{6} =$

7. $7\frac{3}{12} + 4\frac{1}{8} =$

8. $6\frac{7}{8} - 4\frac{2}{9} =$

9. $8\frac{1}{3} + 6\frac{7}{6} =$

10. $5\frac{2}{7} - 3\frac{5}{6} =$

11. $13\frac{4}{21} - 8\frac{2}{3} =$

12. $9\frac{8}{11} + 4\frac{1}{2} =$

13. $5\frac{1}{3} - 3\frac{5}{6} =$

14. $4\frac{3}{10} - 2\frac{9}{12} =$

15. $4\frac{10}{12} - 3\frac{4}{6} =$

16. $7\frac{7}{12} - 3\frac{2}{3} =$

17. $3\frac{15}{18} + 2\frac{4}{12} =$

18. $3\frac{2}{3} + 6\frac{3}{5} =$

Fractions

Multiplying Fractions

$$\text{rewrite} \quad 1\frac{2}{5} \times 2\frac{1}{2} = \frac{7}{5} \times \frac{5}{2} = \frac{35}{10} \text{ or } 3\frac{5}{10} = 3\frac{1}{2}$$
$$\text{rewrite}$$

Solve each problem. Write the answer in simplest form.

1. $10\frac{2}{3} \times 7\frac{1}{8} =$

2. $5\frac{4}{7} \times 1\frac{2}{3} =$

3. $4\frac{5}{6} \times 5\frac{1}{7} =$

4. $\frac{3}{5} \times \frac{15}{18} =$

5. $8\frac{1}{3} \times 6\frac{3}{5} =$

6. $2\frac{11}{13} \times 4\frac{2}{3} =$

7. $5\frac{1}{2} \times \frac{3}{11} =$

8. $3\frac{1}{5} \times 12\frac{1}{2} =$

9. $5\frac{2}{3} \times 8\frac{1}{4} =$

10. $7\frac{2}{7} \times 2\frac{1}{3} =$

11. $1\frac{1}{2} \times 3\frac{1}{5} =$

12. $\frac{2}{3} \times \frac{21}{24} =$

13. $5\frac{3}{5} \times 2\frac{4}{7} =$

14. $7\frac{2}{3} \times 3\frac{1}{2} =$

15. $5\frac{3}{12} \times 2\frac{1}{7} =$

16. $9\frac{1}{3} \times 2\frac{1}{7} =$

17. $2\frac{3}{5} \times 1\frac{1}{4} =$

18. $2\frac{4}{7} \times 2\frac{3}{9} =$

Fractions

Multiplying Fractions

$$\underset{\text{rewrite}}{2\frac{2}{3}} \times 1\frac{1}{4} = \frac{8}{3} \times \frac{5}{4} = \frac{40}{12} = \frac{10}{3} \text{ or } 3\frac{1}{3}$$

Solve each problem. Write the answer in simplest form.

1. $4\frac{1}{4} \times 5\frac{3}{5} =$

2. $3\frac{1}{3} \times 9\frac{3}{4} =$

3. $8\frac{2}{5} \times 3\frac{4}{7} =$

4. $8\frac{1}{3} \times 2\frac{4}{7} =$

5. $7\frac{1}{3} \times 4\frac{1}{2} =$

6. $15\frac{3}{4} \times 6\frac{2}{7} =$

7. $13\frac{1}{3} \times 2\frac{2}{5} =$

8. $5\frac{3}{4} \times 4\frac{4}{5} =$

9. $8\frac{4}{5} \times 2\frac{5}{10} =$

10. $6\frac{2}{9} \times 2\frac{2}{3} =$

11. $3\frac{3}{5} \times 2\frac{7}{9} =$

12. $4\frac{7}{12} \times 6\frac{2}{5} =$

13. $7\frac{1}{8} \times 9\frac{1}{3} =$

14. $4\frac{2}{3} \times 7\frac{1}{2} =$

15. $5\frac{4}{9} \times 2\frac{4}{7} =$

16. $10\frac{1}{2} \times 7\frac{1}{3} =$

17. $3\frac{8}{9} \times 2\frac{1}{5} =$

18. $12\frac{1}{2} \times 8\frac{2}{5} =$

Fractions

Dividing Fractions

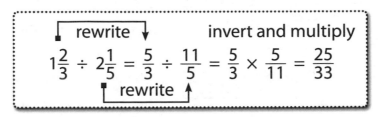

$$1\frac{2}{3} \div 2\frac{1}{5} = \frac{5}{3} \div \frac{11}{5} = \frac{5}{3} \times \frac{5}{11} = \frac{25}{33}$$

rewrite   invert and multiply   rewrite

Solve each problem. Write the answer in simplest form.

1. $6\frac{2}{3} \div 4\frac{4}{9} =$

2. $3\frac{1}{3} \div 1\frac{5}{9} =$

3. $2\frac{7}{10} \div 3\frac{9}{15} =$

4. $4\frac{1}{2} \div 5\frac{1}{4} =$

5. $6\frac{3}{4} \div 2\frac{1}{2} =$

6. $2\frac{2}{6} \div 4\frac{2}{3} =$

7. $5\frac{2}{5} \div 4\frac{1}{2} =$

8. $7\frac{2}{7} \div 2\frac{2}{14} =$

9. $3\frac{1}{2} \div 4\frac{1}{3} =$

10. $2\frac{2}{3} \div 3\frac{4}{10} =$

11. $4\frac{1}{5} \div 3\frac{3}{5} =$

12. $5\frac{3}{5} \div 1\frac{5}{9} =$

13. $4\frac{3}{8} \div 2\frac{1}{12} =$

14. $7\frac{3}{4} \div 1\frac{1}{4} =$

15. $3\frac{3}{4} \div 1\frac{2}{3} =$

16. $3\frac{1}{5} \div 1\frac{6}{10} =$

17. $2\frac{2}{9} \div 4\frac{1}{6} =$

18. $4\frac{3}{5} \div 1\frac{3}{8} =$

Fractions

Dividing Fractions

$$\underset{\text{rewrite}}{\overset{\text{rewrite}}{\downarrow}} \quad \text{invert and multiply}$$

$$1\frac{1}{8} \div 2\frac{1}{6} = \frac{9}{8} \div \frac{13}{6} = \frac{9}{8} \times \frac{6}{13} = \frac{27}{52}$$

Solve each problem. Write the answer in simplest form.

1. $9\frac{1}{6} \div 3\frac{5}{12} =$

2. $9\frac{1}{6} \div 3\frac{8}{12} =$

3. $7\frac{1}{2} \div 8\frac{3}{4} =$

4. $5\frac{1}{2} \div 8\frac{4}{5} =$

5. $5\frac{4}{5} \div 1\frac{8}{15} =$

6. $9\frac{1}{5} \div 2\frac{3}{10} =$

7. $7\frac{4}{5} \div 1\frac{3}{10} =$

8. $7\frac{1}{9} \div 2\frac{2}{3} =$

9. $8\frac{4}{5} \div 1\frac{1}{15} =$

10. $8\frac{2}{5} \div 2\frac{1}{10} =$

11. $5\frac{3}{5} \div 1\frac{6}{10} =$

12. $6\frac{1}{3} \div 2\frac{1}{6} =$

13. $11\frac{3}{4} \div 5\frac{1}{2} =$

14. $8\frac{3}{5} \div 2\frac{7}{10} =$

15. $3\frac{5}{7} \div 3\frac{13}{14} =$

16. $3\frac{3}{4} \div 3\frac{1}{8} =$

17. $9\frac{3}{7} \div 5\frac{10}{14} =$

18. $5\frac{1}{6} \div 2\frac{1}{12} =$

Fractions

Mixed Practice with Fractions

Solve each problem. Write the answer in simplest form.

1. $5\frac{1}{3} \div 2\frac{4}{12} =$

2. $7\frac{1}{2} + 6\frac{3}{4} =$

3. $4\frac{4}{5} \times 3\frac{3}{4} =$

4. $15\frac{3}{4} \times 3\frac{3}{7} =$

5. $\frac{3}{5} \div \frac{4}{5} =$

6. $5\frac{3}{5} + 8\frac{1}{4} =$

7. $11\frac{1}{7} - 7\frac{5}{6} =$

8. $7\frac{1}{2} - 2\frac{3}{7} =$

9. $7\frac{3}{5} + 4\frac{7}{8} =$

10. $7\frac{1}{2} \div 4\frac{1}{6} =$

11. $4\frac{6}{3} + 6\frac{2}{3} =$

12. $4\frac{2}{15} - 1\frac{11}{12} =$

13. $\frac{7}{8} \times \frac{3}{14} =$

14. $9\frac{3}{5} \div 3\frac{6}{10} =$

15. $15\frac{5}{6} + 3\frac{4}{9} =$

16. $8 - 3\frac{2}{7} =$

17. $6\frac{6}{15} - 2\frac{4}{15} =$

18. $5\frac{5}{8} \times 5\frac{1}{3} =$

19. $8\frac{6}{30} + 6\frac{5}{15} =$

20. $3\frac{1}{2} \times 8\frac{4}{5} =$

21. $4\frac{2}{5} \div 3\frac{3}{10} =$

Fractions

Problem Solving with Fractions

Solve each problem. Show your work. Write the answer in simplest form.

1. Katie wants to make muffins for a school party. The recipe calls for $5\frac{1}{2}$ cups of flour. A 16-ounce bag of flour contains 2 cups. How many bags of flour must Katie purchase to make the cookies?

2. A banana bread recipe calls for $1\frac{2}{3}$ cups of flour, $1\frac{1}{3}$ cups of sugar, $\frac{2}{3}$ cups of sliced bananas, and $2\frac{2}{3}$ cups of walnuts. How many cups of ingredients are needed to make the banana bread?

3. If $2\frac{1}{2}$ pounds of pecans cost $2.10 and $2\frac{1}{3}$ pounds of almonds cost $2.60, which nut is less expensive per pound?

4. Marta brought her lunch to school 15 days out of the month of May. Out of these days, she brought carrot sticks $\frac{2}{5}$ of the time. How many days did she bring carrot sticks in May?

5. Josie is making fruit salad for a party. She bought $1\frac{1}{2}$ pounds of apples, $1\frac{3}{4}$ pounds of cherries, and $2\frac{2}{3}$ pounds of grapes. How many pounds of fruit did Josie buy in all?

6. A cake recipe calls for $\frac{1}{2}$ cups of flour, $\frac{2}{3}$ cup of water, $\frac{1}{5}$ cup of salt. How many cups of ingredients are needed to make the cake?

Decimals

Writing Fractions as Decimals

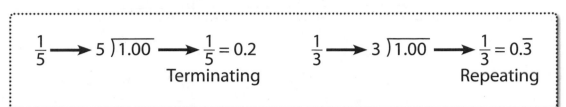

$\frac{1}{5}$ ⟶ $5\overline{)1.00}$ ⟶ $\frac{1}{5} = 0.2$
Terminating

$\frac{1}{3}$ ⟶ $3\overline{)1.00}$ ⟶ $\frac{1}{3} = 0.\overline{3}$
Repeating

Write each fraction as a decimal. Draw a line above repeating numbers in decimals.

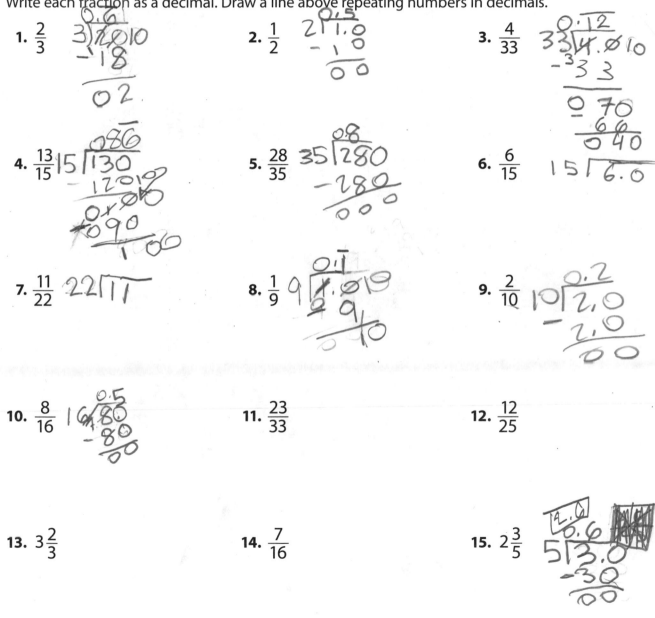

1. $\frac{2}{3}$

2. $\frac{1}{2}$

3. $\frac{4}{33}$

4. $\frac{13}{15}$

5. $\frac{28}{35}$

6. $\frac{6}{15}$

7. $\frac{11}{22}$

8. $\frac{1}{9}$

9. $\frac{2}{10}$

10. $\frac{8}{16}$

11. $\frac{23}{33}$

12. $\frac{12}{25}$

13. $3\frac{2}{3}$

14. $\frac{7}{16}$

15. $2\frac{3}{5}$

Decimals

Writing Fractions as Decimals

Write each fraction as a decimal. Draw a line above repeating numbers in decimals.

1. $\frac{9}{36}$

2. $\frac{8}{15}$

3. $\frac{30}{45}$

4. $\frac{19}{57}$

5. $\frac{45}{72}$

6. $\frac{21}{36}$

7. $\frac{10}{60}$

8. $\frac{32}{36}$

9. $\frac{56}{63}$

10. $\frac{13}{39}$

11. $\frac{5}{10}$

12. $\frac{12}{18}$

13. $\frac{8}{24}$

14. $\frac{56}{64}$

15. $\frac{48}{74}$

16. $\frac{6}{22}$

17. $\frac{16}{72}$

18. $\frac{35}{55}$

19. $\frac{6}{40}$

20. $\frac{4}{36}$

21. $\frac{7}{48}$

Decimals

Rounding Decimals

> Round 15.443 to the nearest tenth.
> 15.4④3 ⟶ 4 < 5 therefore 15.443 = 15.4
>
> Round 22.72 to the nearest whole number.
> 22.⑦2 ⟶ 7 > 5 therefore 22.72 = 23

Round each decimal to the nearest whole number.

1. 13.398   **2.** 29.88   **3.** 34.87   **4.** 42.575

5. 15.91   **6.** 78.612   **7.** 4.32   **8.** 53.937

9. 7.4344   **10.** 53.409   **11.** 4.98   **12.** 1.19

Round each decimal to the nearest tenth.

1. 1.53   **2.** 1.4578   **3.** 32.277   **4.** 3.545

5. 2.708   **6.** 342.38   **7.** 33.897   **8.** 11.343

9. 3.869   **10.** 111.111   **11.** 414.74   **12.** 41.564

Round each decimal to the nearest hundredth.

1. 218.455   **2.** 21.564   **3.** 2.6323   **4.** 241.565

5. 5.5555   **6.** 212.635   **7.** 430.234   **8.** 12.1212

9. 12.7639   **10.** 129.414   **11.** 6.435   **12.** 7.34127

Decimals

Multiplying and Dividing by Powers of 10

$12.56 \times 1\underline{0} \longrightarrow 12.56 \longrightarrow 125.6$
Move the decimal point to the right one place.

$12.56 \times 1\underline{00} \longrightarrow 12.56 \longrightarrow 1256$
Move the decimal point to the right two places.

$12.565 \times 1\underline{000} \longrightarrow 12.565 \longrightarrow 12565$
Move the decimal point to the right three places.

$125.6 \div 1\underline{000} \longrightarrow 125.6 \longrightarrow 0.1256$
Move the decimal point to the left three places.

Solve each problem. Show your work.

1. $78 \times 100 =$

2. $0.042 \div 100 =$

3. $2.7 \times 10 =$

4. $0.00198 \div 100 =$

5. $2.7453 \times 1000 =$

6. $3.581 \div 100,000 =$

7. $5123.23 \div 10,000 =$

8. $2.755 \times 10 =$

9. $57,450 \div 100 =$

10. $0.0442 \times 100,000 =$

11. $0.000999 \times 1,000 =$

12. $4.342 \times 100,000 =$

13. $67.009 \div 1000 =$

14. $40,750 \times 1000 =$

15. $3.456 \times 10 =$

16. $345.682 \div 100 =$

17. $32.949 \times 100 =$

18. $35.98 \times 10,000 =$

19. $0.51 \div 10,000 =$

20. $23,098 \div 10,000 =$

Decimals

Adding Decimals

$$12.2 + 5.25 = \begin{array}{r} 12.20 \\ +\ 5.25 \\ \hline 17.45 \end{array}$$

Solve each problem.

1. $9.87 + 2.87 =$

2. $5.02 + 8.2 =$

3. $2.49 + 4.73 =$

4. $6.41 + 2.734 + 8.41 =$

5. $2.934 + 231.6 =$

6. $121.9 + 0.736 =$

7. $43.56 + 85.7 =$

8. $13.238 + 4.82 =$

9. $15.76 + 25.23 + 3.9 =$

10. $6.41 + 3.99 =$

11. $6.3 + 9.124 + 2.34 =$

12. $5.97 + 4.87 + 3.908 =$

13. $13.39 + 7.4 =$

14. $4.63 + 23.5 + 5.0 =$

15. $3.456 + 2.894 =$

16. $3.64 + 5.32 =$

17. $5.7 + 5.34 + 4.78 =$

18. $3.5 + 8.4 =$

19. $0.034 + 10.51 =$

20. $123.415 + 6.876 =$

Decimals

Adding Decimals

$$7.5 + 6.12 = \quad \begin{array}{r} 7.50 \\ + \ 6.12 \\ \hline 13.62 \end{array}$$

Solve each problem.

1. $40.14 + 12.53 + 5.6 =$ **2.** $3.43 + 5.45 =$

3. $3.59 + 2.08 =$ **4.** $17.34 + 6.45 =$

5. $2.15 + 4.25 =$ **6.** $108.7 + 0.489 =$

7. $31.71 + 324.95 =$ **8.** $121.356 + 80.52 =$

9. $5.37 + 7.37 =$ **10.** $7.22 + 3.41 =$

11. $2.6 + 45.54 + 3.65 =$ **12.** $6.29 + 8.83 + 6.332 =$

13. $5.4 + 7.38 + 6.21 =$ **14.** $8.45 + 23.20 + 5.34 =$

15. $5.44 + 3.34 + 6.30 =$ **16.** $2.312 + 5.371 =$

17. $12.52 + 8.32 =$ **18.** $321.595 + 3.45 =$

19. $0.012 + 25.08 =$ **20.** $17.121 + 5.34 =$

Decimals

Subtracting Decimals

$$13.2 - 4.10 = \begin{array}{r} 13.20 \\ -\ 4.10 \\ \hline 9.10 \end{array}$$

Solve each problem.

1. $4.239 - 0.06 =$

2. $51.23 - 14.45 =$

3. $16.3 - 12.4 =$

4. $452.82 - 127.36 =$

5. $62.1 - 33.29 =$

6. $75.034 - 22.439 =$

7. $76.34 - 47.30 =$

8. $34.32 - 12.43 =$

9. $435.34 - 345.34 =$

10. $756.98 - 32.43 =$

11. $513.43 - 305.342 =$

12. $65.9 - 33.2 =$

13. $21.73 - 16.43 =$

14. $121.32 - 19.34 =$

15. $23.28 - 0.552 - 1.2 =$

16. $8.64 - 0.476 =$

17. $13.2 - 6.7 =$

18. $21.32 - 4.28 =$

19. $35.63 - 0.021 =$

20. $485.02 - 332.86 =$

Name _____   Date _____

Decimals

Subtracting Decimals

$$10.5 - 3.21 = \begin{array}{r} 10.50 \\ -\ 3.21 \\ \hline 7.29 \end{array}$$

Solve each problem.

1. $43{,}289.56 - 28{,}125.87 =$

2. $756.84 - 31.343 =$

3. $34.34 - 23.19 =$

4. $4.7 - 2.3 =$

5. $95.87 - 52.45 =$

6. $72.72 - 43.562 =$

7. $85.76 - 34.65 =$

8. $7.435 - 0.0345 =$

9. $345.24 - 159.24 =$

10. $54.68 - 23.76 =$

11. $74.71 - 61.92 =$

12. $84.8 - 44.87 =$

13. $857.44 - 22.39 =$

14. $93.76 - 8.67 =$

15. $233.23 - 6.45 =$

16. $6.56 - 0.654 =$

17. $43.5 - 0.015 - 3.2 =$

18. $39.43 - 15.34 =$

19. $56.4 - 0.043 =$

20. $954.34 - 657.56 =$

CD-104315 • © Carson-Dellosa

Decimals

Multiplying Decimals

$$
\begin{array}{r}
0.3 \\
\times\ 0.12 \\
\hline
0.036
\end{array}
$$

(0.3)(0.12) — 3 decimal places ⟶

Solve each problem. Show your work.

1. (0.6)(0.022) =

2. (0.012)(0.7) =

3. (3.2)(0.65) =

4. 0.07×0.4 =

5. (0.02)(1.2) =

6. 0.03×0.7 =

7. (0.5)(0.2) =

8. (2.2)(0.22) =

9. (0.12)(0.04) =

10. 0.06×0.07 =

11. (0.11)(0.07) =

12. (0.13)(0.02) =

13. (0.7)(0.07) =

14. (0.5)(0.05) =

15. 0.5×0.06 =

16. (0.012)(1.2) =

17. (0.8)(0.005) =

18. 0.25×0.07 =

19. (0.9)(0.002) =

20. (0.9)(0.9) =

Decimals

Multiplying Decimals Using a Calculator

Solve each problem. Use a calculator.

1. $(12.3)(5.81)(0.06) =$

2. $(0.042)(0.006) =$

3. $(0.34)(0.12)(0.104) =$

4. $(8.9)(0.11)(3.09) =$

5. $(15.92)(0.4)(0.32) =$

6. $(0.004)(6) =$

7. $(6.4)(0.3) =$

8. $(0.4)(0.232) =$

9. $(5.12)(6) =$

10. $(10.89)(0.221) =$

11. $(3.28)(12.8) =$

12. $(0.004)(0.0004)(0.04) =$

13. $(0.016)(3.8) =$

14. $(0.007)(0.6)(0.05) =$

15. $(3.806)(10.01) =$

16. $(340)(0.02) =$

17. $(0.8)(0.342)(0.02) =$

18. $(2.09)(0.005) =$

19. $(0.05)(0.15)(0.002) =$

20. $(5.4)(0.645)(0.07) =$

21. $(0.7)(0.8) =$

22. $(9)(0.03)(0.2) =$

CD-104315 • © Carson-Dellosa

Decimals

Dividing Decimals

Solve each problem. Use mental math.

1. $0.036 \div 0.6 =$

2. $0.55 \div 0.005 =$

3. $7.2 \div 1.2 =$

4. $100 \div 0.01 =$

5. $4.8 \div 0.06 =$

6. $0.0027 \div 0.9 =$

7. $1.69 \div 0.13 =$

8. $0.108 \div 0.09 =$

9. $0.44 \div 0.4 =$

10. $1.21 \div .11 =$

11. $8.4 \div 0.12 =$

12. $0.064 \div 0.8 =$

13. $3.6 \div 0.009 =$

14. $0.0054 \div 0.006 =$

15. $0.012 \div 0.3 =$

16. $14.4 \div 1.2 =$

17. $0.56 \div 0.008 =$

18. $2.6 \div 0.02 =$

19. $0.072 \div 0.08 =$

20. $6.3 \div 0.06 =$

21. $0.32 \div 0.008 =$

22. $0.132 \div 0.012 =$

Decimals

Dividing Decimals Using a Calculator

Solve each problem. Use a calculator.

1. $6.3056 \div 4.2 =$

2. $7.57 \div 0.1 =$

3. $3.56 \div 2.5 =$

4. $0.493 \div 0.33 =$

5. $8.565 \div 2 =$

6. $0.0135 \div 4.5 =$

7. $40.78 \div 0.2 =$

8. $9.51 \div 3.03 =$

9. $12.63 \div 0.9 =$

10. $9.414 \div 3.3 =$

11. $1.35 \div 0.07 =$

12. $16.73 \div 0.12 =$

13. $3.605 \div 3.2 =$

14. $0.1827 \div 0.09 =$

15. $12.264 \div 5.6 =$

16. $6.65 \div 2.4 =$

17. $2.34 \div 0.012 =$

18. $0.576 \div 4.1 =$

19. $15.8 \div 0.09 =$

20. $8.176 \div 3.2 =$

21. $0.0224 \div 3.6 =$

22. $21.5 \div 0.05 =$

Decimals

Mixed Practice with Decimals

Solve each problem.

1. $725.987 - 231.155 =$

2. $2.34 \div 1.6 =$

3. $42.25 + 53.5 =$

4. $2.62 \div 0.54 =$

5. $(7.8)(1.03) =$

6. $23.65 \div 22.5 =$

7. $872.6 \div 2.4 =$

8. $12.828 + 10.548 =$

9. $1.32 \div 1.8 =$

10. $0.6 + 0.09 + 1.75 =$

11. $5.2 \div 1.2 =$

12. $87.21 - 13.98 + 22.23 =$

13. $13.58 - 7.2 =$

14. $432.42 - 327.89 =$

15. $(3.2)(3.065) =$

16. $(12.2)(34.9) =$

17. $1{,}343.32 - 1{,}032.90 =$

18. $(0.04)(0.24)(1.4) =$

19. $65.78 + 54.90 =$

20. $21.7 - 15.9 =$

21. $(2.5)(3.3)(.33) =$

22. $6.77 + 0.05 =$

Decimals

Mixed Practice with Decimals

Solve each problem.

1. $3.6 \div 0.3 =$

2. $15.54 - 11.56 + 33.43 =$

3. $20.59 + 44.5 =$

4. $(1.3)(3.04)(5.46) =$

5. $(4.3)(3.59) =$

6. $44.34 \div 32.76 =$

7. $34.96 \div 3.549 =$

8. $4.33 \div 0.3 =$

9. $7.569 \div 3.459 =$

10. $154.34 + 42.98 =$

11. $17.546 + 5.0958 =$

12. $843.21 - 452.03 =$

13. $15.51 - 8.34 =$

14. $23.565 + 28.403 =$

15. $(5.5)(4.304) =$

16. $545.825 - 137.405 =$

17. $43.5 - 14.2 =$

18. $(23.4)(3.9) =$

19. $0.8 + 0.07 + 3.73 =$

20. $1,350.65 - 253.42 =$

21. $(5.5)(2.6)(4.0) =$

22. $8.37 \div 4.50 =$

CD-104315 • © Carson-Dellosa

Decimals

Problem Solving with Decimals

John and Jason went to a grocery store and bought some sandwiches for $4.95, a gallon of fruit juice for $3.31, and a bag of carrots for $3.15. How much did they spend altogether?

$$\$4.95 + \$3.31 + \$3.15 = \begin{array}{r} \$4.95 \\ \$3.31 \\ + \ \$3.15 \\ \hline \mathbf{\$11.41} \end{array} \right\} \text{ each grocery item}$$

$\mathbf{\$11.41}$ total

Solve each problem. Show your work.

1. George went to the store to buy a pair of pants. The pair of pants that George picked out cost $45.00. If the price of the pants was reduced by $10.85, how much will George pay?

2. Gary spent $13.41 on clothes in January, $25.95 in February, and $31.50 in March. Altogether, how much money did he spend on clothes in these months?

3. Jesse buys a shirt for $32.95 and a pair of shoes for $46.25. How much money does Jesse spend in all?

4. Heather bought some new fishing equipment. She bought a tackle box for $24.95, a fishing pole for $58.49, a life jacket for $37.75, and an ice chest for $57.41. How much money did Heather spend on her equipment?

5. Marisol and Kurt are making sandwiches. The ingredients for the sandwiches cost $6.07. The sandwiches from the store cost $8.55. How much money are they saving?

6. Cindy buys a shirt for $26.70, a pair of jeans for $47.55, a jacket for $25.54, and a hat for $20.11. How much does Cindy spend in all?

Decimals

Writing Decimals as Fractions

Terminating Decimals	Repeating Decimals
$0.50 = \dfrac{50}{100} = \dfrac{1}{2}$	$x = 0.6666\ldots = 0.\overline{6}$ $10x = 6.\overline{6}$ $\underline{x = 0.\overline{6}}$ $9x = 6$ $x = \dfrac{6}{9}$ or $\dfrac{2}{3}$

Write each decimal as a fraction. Write the answer in simplest form.

1. 0.6875

2. $0.\overline{35}$

3. 0.212

4. $0.4\overline{8}$

5. 0.625

6. 0.54

7. 0.44

8. $0.\overline{29}$

9. 0.775

10. $0.\overline{33}$

11. 0.562

12. $0.91\overline{6}$

CD-104315 • © Carson-Dellosa

Decimals

Writing Decimals as Fractions

Write each decimal as a fraction. Write the answer in simplest form.

1. 0.345

2. 0.12

3. 0.555

4. 0.300

5. 0.942

6. 0.24

7. 0.34$\overline{58}$

8. 0.28

9. 0.13$\overline{4}$

10. 0.59

11. 0.34

12. 0.342

13. 0.708

14. 0.144

15. 0.65

16. 0.920

17. 0.33$\overline{4}$

18. 0.438

19. 0.378

20. 0.82

21. 0.2052

22. 0.6$\overline{22}$

Ratios, Proportions, and Percents

Ratios

$$3 \text{ to } 12 \longrightarrow \frac{3}{12} = \frac{1}{4}$$

$$25:30 \longrightarrow \frac{25}{30} = \frac{5}{6}$$

$$5 \text{ out of } 15 \longrightarrow \frac{5}{15} = \frac{1}{3}$$

Write each ratio as a fraction. Write the answer in simplest form.

1. 66 to 40

2. 130 to 112

3. 110:112

4. 65:35

5. 21 to 84

6. 66:166

7. 30 to 323

8. 197 to 17

9. 18 to 76

10. 19 to 27

11. 0.12:1.44

12. 167 to 132

13. 50 to 90

14. 175 to 200

15. 65:115

16. 113:226

Ratios, Proportions, and Percents

Ratios

$$2 \text{ to } 8 \longrightarrow \frac{2}{8} = \frac{1}{4}$$

$$35 : 20 \longrightarrow \frac{35}{20} = \frac{7}{4}$$

$$5 \text{ out of } 25 \longrightarrow \frac{5}{25} = \frac{1}{5}$$

Write each ratio as a fraction. Write the answer in simplest form.

1. 20 to 70

2. 14 to 43

3. 121:108

4. 51:102

5. 34 out of 82

6. 112:224

7. 21 to 45

8. 40: 231

9. 19 to 84

10. 237 to 32

11. 0.13 out of 1.69

12. 171 to 132

13. 150 to 275

14. 60 to 116

15. 12 out of 133

16. 50:125

Ratios, Proportions, and Percents

Proportions

$$\frac{2}{6} = \frac{x}{18}$$

$$2 \cdot 18 = 6x$$

$$\frac{36}{6} = \frac{6x}{6}$$

$$6 = x$$

Solve each proportion. Use cross–products.

1. $\frac{1}{4} = \frac{x}{8}$

2. $\frac{20}{30} = \frac{5}{x}$

3. $\frac{18}{24} = \frac{12}{x}$

4. $\frac{80}{x} = \frac{48}{20}$

5. $\frac{5}{5} = \frac{5x}{5}$

6. $\frac{15}{45} = \frac{3}{x}$

7. $\frac{1.8}{x} = \frac{3.6}{2.8}$

8. $\frac{8}{x} = \frac{5}{2}$

9. $\frac{8}{6} = \frac{x}{27}$

10. $\frac{144}{6} = \frac{6x}{6}$

11. $\frac{x}{3} = \frac{8}{8}$

12. $\frac{36}{12} = \frac{x}{6}$

13. $\frac{0.14}{0.07} = \frac{x}{1.5}$

14. $\frac{6}{x} = \frac{6}{4}$

15. $\frac{4}{5} = \frac{x}{5}$

16. $\frac{16}{48} = \frac{x}{50}$

Ratios, Proportions, and Percents

Problem Solving with Proportions

If 3 liters of juice cost $3.75, how much does 9 liters cost?

$$\frac{\text{liters}}{\text{cost}} = \frac{3}{3.75} = \frac{9}{x}$$

$$3x = 3.75 \cdot 9$$

$$\frac{3x}{3} = \frac{33.75}{3} \qquad x = 11.25$$
$$\qquad\qquad\qquad\qquad \text{9 liters cost } \$11.25$$

Solve each problem. Round each answer to the nearest cent.

1. If 3 square feet of fabric cost $3.75, what would 7 square feet cost?

2. A 12-ounce bottle of soap costs $2.50. How many ounces would be in a bottle that costs $3.75?

3. Four pounds of apples cost $5.00. How much would 10 pounds of apples cost?

4. A 12-ounce can of lemonade costs $1.32. How much would a 16-ounce can of lemonade cost?

5. J & S Jewelry company bought 800 bracelets for $450.00. How much did each bracelet cost?

6. A dozen peaches costs $3.60. How much did each peach cost?

7. A 32-pound box of cantaloupe costs $24.40. How much would a 12-pound box cost?

8. If a 10-pound turkey costs $20.42, how much would a 21-pound turkey cost?

Ratios, Proportions, and Percents

Percents

```
Fraction to percent              Decimal to percent

  1  ────►  1     x
  ─         ─  =  ───           0.425 ────► 0.425 = 42.5%
  2         2     100
            2x = 100            When converting a decimal
            x = 50              to a percent, move the decimal
            1                   two places to the right.
            ─ = 50%
            2
```

Write each fraction or decimal as a percent. Round each answer to the nearest hundredth.

1. $\dfrac{7}{21}$

2. 10.8

3. 12.392

4. 523.32

5. 2.3839

6. $\dfrac{12}{19}$

7. $\dfrac{5}{46}$

8. $\dfrac{11}{23}$

9. $\dfrac{4}{13}$

10. 2.32

11. 17.45

12. 5.293

  CD-104315 • © Carson-Dellosa

Ratios, Proportions, and Percents

Percents

$$60\% = \frac{60}{100} = \frac{6}{10} = \frac{3}{5}$$

$$51.5\% = \frac{51.5}{100} = \frac{515}{1,000} = \frac{103}{200}$$

Write each percent as a fraction. Write each fraction as a percent. Write the answers that are fractions in simplest form.

1. 0.68%

2. 33.8%

3. 8.6%

4. 21.98%

5. 4.934%

6. $7\frac{4}{21}$

7. 5.75%

8. $3\frac{34}{88}$

9. $4\frac{5}{46}$

10. $2\frac{5}{7}$

11. 364.69%

12. $21\frac{7}{32}$

13. 12.4%

14. $6\frac{1}{2}$

15. $1\frac{3}{4}$

16. 2.98%

Ratios, Proportions, and Percents

Percents

$$50\% \text{ of } 60 = \underline{\hspace{1cm}}$$
$$\frac{50}{100} = \frac{x}{60}$$
$$100x = 3000$$
$$x = 30$$

$$\underline{\hspace{1cm}}\% \text{ of } 40 = 20$$
$$\frac{x}{100} = \frac{20}{40}$$
$$40x = 2000$$
$$x = 50 \quad 50\%$$

$$40\% \text{ of } \underline{\hspace{1cm}} = 30$$
$$\frac{40}{100} = \frac{30}{x}$$
$$40x = 3000$$
$$x = 75$$

Solve each problem.

1. 20% of 15 =

2. 30% of 60 =

3. 15% of 75 =

4. 37% of 65 =

5. 44% of 40 =

6. _____% of 35 = 15

7. _____% of 70 = 20

8. _____% of 48 = 8

9. _____% of 65 = 33

10. _____% of 9 = 4

11. 12% of _____ = 76

12. 65% of _____ = 80

13. 20% of _____ = 75

14. 45% of _____ = 150

15. 22% of _____ = 34

16. 50% of _____ = 52

Ratios, Proportions, and Percents

Problem Solving with Percents

> A baseball team played 30 games and won 50% of them. How many games did the team win?
>
> $$50\% \text{ of } 30 = \underline{\hspace{1cm}}$$
> $$\frac{50}{100} = \frac{x}{30}$$
> $$100x = 1500$$
> $$x = 15 \text{ games}$$

Solve each problem. Show your work.

1. In a group of 35 students, 7 have yellow socks. What percentage of the students have yellow socks?

2. A test has 60 questions. Fred answers 75% of them correctly. How many problems does Fred answer correctly?

3. A football team plays 25 games. They win 32% of them. How many games does the team win?

4. The regular price of a pair of pants is $38.00. The pants are discounted 35%. How much do the pants cost after the discount is applied?

5. A store was having a sale on books. The book Bart wants is priced at $19.00. He has a coupon for 30% off. How much does the book cost after the coupn is applied?

6. Lisa went to a restaurant and gave the waiter a 15% tip. If the price of her meal was $10.25, how much did Lisa tip the waiter?

7. Emily bought a new car that cost $22,000. The car was 93% of the list price. How much was the list price?

Integers

Adding Integers with Like Signs

$$\underbrace{5 + 5}_{\text{2 positives}} = 10 \text{ (positive)} \qquad \underbrace{(^-3) + (^-10)}_{\text{2 negatives}} = ^-13 \text{ (negative)}$$

Solve each problem.

1. $(^-13) + (^-34) + (^-67) =$

2. $90 + 52 =$

3. $(^-12) + (^-7) =$

4. $5 + 6 =$

5. $32 + 53 =$

6. $23 + 54 + 56 =$

7. $(^-34) + (^-76) =$

8. $142 + 374 =$

9. $(^-42) + (^-36) + (^-22) =$

10. $13 + 45 + 84 =$

11. $(^-35) + (^-38) =$

12. $45 + 8 =$

13. $(^-16) + (^-16) + (^-16) =$

14. $15 + 41 + 7 =$

15. $(^-60) + (^-39) =$

16. $(^-2) + (^-124) + (^-438) =$

17. $(^-12) + (^-34) + (^-46) + (^-261) =$

18. $12 + 45 + 332 =$

19. $(^-16) + (^-16) =$

20. $23 + 72 =$

Integers

Adding Integers with Like Signs

| $\underbrace{6 + 6}_{\text{2 positives}} = 12 \text{ (positive)}$ | $\underbrace{(^-3) + (^-4)}_{\text{2 negatives}} = ^-7 \text{ (negative)}$ |

Solve each problem.

1. $(^-21) + (^-22) + (^-41) =$

2. $50 + 82 =$

3. $(^-14) + (^-9) =$

4. $7 + 8 =$

5. $27 + 53 =$

6. $50 + 63 + 82 =$

7. $(^-21) + (^-34) =$

8. $36 + 57 + 58 =$

9. $213 + 375 =$

10. $(^-21) + (^-41) + (^-55) =$

11. $(^-163) + (^-238) =$

12. $(^-14) + (^-34) + (^-67) =$

13. $(^-23) + (^-48) =$

14. $(^-21) + (^-59) + (^-828) =$

15. $29 + 67 =$

16. $21 + 22 + 23 =$

17. $34 + 46 =$

18. $(^-13) + (^-65) + (^-78) + (^-332) =$

19. $(^-20) + (^-68) =$

20. $51 + 87 + 527 =$

Integers

Adding Integers with Unlike Signs

$$5 + (^-13) = ^-8 \qquad\qquad ^-12 + 14 = 2$$
$$5 - 13 = ^-8 \qquad\qquad 14 - 12 = 2$$

Solve each problem.

1. $8 + (^-11) =$

2. $^-73 + 12 =$

3. $^-17 + 6 =$

4. $310 + (^-673) =$

5. $56 + (^-7) =$

6. $^-1{,}565 + 576 =$

7. $^-17 + 33 =$

8. $17{,}985 + (^-22{,}581) =$

9. $^-213 + 56 =$

10. $^-563{,}937 + 76{,}412 =$

11. $^-167 + 121 =$

12. $^-12 + 9 =$

13. $48 + (^-56) =$

14. $45{,}908 + (^-12{,}921) =$

15. $^-61 + 61 =$

16. $^-19 + 39 =$

17. $^-34{,}132 + 81{,}323 =$

18. $57 + (^-90) =$

19. $34 + (^-34) =$

20. $642 + (^-423) =$

Integers

Adding Integers with Unlike Signs

$$4 + (^-12) = ^-8 \qquad\qquad ^-10 + 14 = 4$$
$$4 - 12 = ^-8 \qquad\qquad 14 - 10 = 4$$

Solve each problem.

1. $24 + (^-67) =$

2. $^-6{,}607 + 4{,}362 =$

3. $^-194 + 635 =$

4. $^-23{,}895 + 5{,}863 =$

5. $321 + (^-494) =$

6. $714 + (^-6{,}976) =$

7. $^-43 + 68 =$

8. $131{,}985 + (^-454{,}202) =$

9. $^-343 + 439 =$

10. $^-112{,}956 + 564{,}258 =$

11. $^-595 + 630 =$

12. $67{,}888 + (^-78{,}952) =$

13. $55{,}980 + (^-42{,}278) =$

14. $^-64{,}412 + 73{,}651 =$

15. $^-99 + 94 =$

16. $88 + (^-34) =$

17. $^-84{,}154 + 89{,}343 =$

18. $34{,}139 + (^-56{,}913) =$

19. $^-73 + 25 =$

20. $850 + (^-828) =$

Integers

Subtracting Integers

$$6 - 10 = 6 + (^-10) = ^-4 \qquad 6 - (^-10) = 6 + 10 = 16$$

Add the opposite   Add the opposite

Solve each problem.

1. $^-8 - 3 =$

2. $56 - (^-65) =$

3. $^-52 - (^-34) =$

4. $^-19 - (^-13) =$

5. $42 - 23 =$

6. $77 - 22 =$

7. $17 - 26 =$

8. $^-594 - (^-73) =$

9. $^-117 - 29 =$

10. $^-749 - 629 =$

11. $19 - (^-342) =$

12. $2{,}567 - (^-492) =$

13. $5{,}762 - 2{,}144 =$

14. $121 - 154 =$

15. $^-8 - (^-27) =$

16. $^-87 - 129 =$

17. $45 - 75 =$

18. $688 - 456 =$

19. $187 - (^-48) =$

20. $157 - (^-452) =$

Name _____ Date _____

Integers

Subtracting Integers

Solve each problem.

1. $7 - 15 =$

2. $319 - (^-749) =$

3. $^-18 - 6 =$

4. $^-60 - 17 =$

5. $^-45 - (^-45) =$

6. $^-54 - (^-95) =$

$-54 + 95 =$

7. $^-154 - 56 =$

8. $^-625 - 127 =$

9. $^-21 - (^-45) =$

10. $564 - (^-373) =$

$6,593 (^-4,132)$

11. $3 - (^-67) =$

12. $6,593 - (^-4,132) =$

13. $0 - 15 =$

14. $108,762 - (^-95,671) =$

15. $^-3 - (^-7) =$

16. $^-9,774 - 8,834 =$

17. $^-5 - (^-67) =$

18. $^-23 - 56 =$

19. $^-44 - 57 =$

20. $^-475,824 - (^-153,198) =$

21. $^-36 - 69 =$

22. $^-934 - (^-672) =$

23. $^-630,805 - (^-512,156) =$

24. $899,342 - (^-392,231) =$

Integers

Adding and Subtracting Integers

Solve each problem.

1. ⁻233 – (⁻233) =

2. ⁻16 – (⁻38) =

3. ⁻19 – 4 =

4. 0 – 17 =

5. ⁻13 + 26 =

6. ⁻59 – 43 =

7. 31 – (⁻8) =

8. 43 + (⁻56) – 78 =

9. ⁻16 + 9 =

10. ⁻8 + (⁻5) =

11. ⁻9 – (⁻24) =

12. ⁻103 + (⁻575) =

13. ⁻78 – 65 =

14. 71 + (⁻18) =

15. 12 + (⁻7) =

16. 0 – (⁻9) =

17. 109 – (⁻53) =

18. 91 – 157 – (⁻33) =

19. ⁻129 + ⁻645 – (⁻13) =

20. ⁻17 + 436 + (⁻642) =

21. ⁻534 – (⁻454) + (⁻58) =

22. ⁻98 – (⁻126) + 19 =

23. 509 – 343 =

24. 24 + (⁻64) =

Integers

Multiplying Integers

$(3)(3) = 9$ $(^-2)(^-3) = 6$ $(-3)(3) = -9$ $(-2)(3) = -6$
Like signs = Positive   Unlike signs = Negative

Solve each problem.

1. $(33)(^-123)(12) =$

2. $(^-434)(^-7) =$

3. $(15)(^-4) =$

4. $(^-5)(^-28)(^-23) =$

5. $(30)(5) =$

6. $(13)(^-28) =$

7. $(^-72)(43) =$

8. $(^-3)(9) =$

9. $(56)(12) =$

10. $(14)(^-33)(2) =$

11. $(32)(^-48) =$

12. $(20)(^-3)(23)(^-3) =$

13. $(^-39)(^-58) =$

14. $(12)(^-12)(2)(^-33) =$

15. $(^-20)(^-10)(2)(3) =$

16. $(37)(^-90) =$

17. $(121)(^-10)(21) =$

18. $(^-9)(^-88)(^-7) =$

19. $(^-13)(^-13) =$

20. $(^-32)(^-22)(^-45) =$

Integers

Multiplying Integers

$(3)(4) = 12$ $(^-3)(^-5) = 15$ $(^-3)(2) = ^-6$ $(^-2)(5) = ^-10$

Like signs = Positive   Unlike signs = Negative

Solve each problem.

1. $(8)(^-99)(^-22)(^-7) =$

2. $(^-9)(^-82)(^-7) =$

3. $(^-7)(3) =$

4. $(^-6)(^-9) =$

5. $(^-10)(^-5)(^-3) =$

6. $(5)(^-4)(^-3) =$

7. $(^-7)(^-2)(^-5) =$

8. $(^-7)(^-14)(144) =$

9. $(^-17)(^-2) =$

10. $(^-2)(^-13)(^-4) =$

11. $(^-8)(^-9) =$

12. $(^-1)(22)(^-33)(44) =$

13. $(21)(^-22) =$

14. $(^-85)(^-215) =$

15. $(4)(111)(^-1) =$

16. $(213)(4)(18) =$

17. $(^-19)(^-38) =$

18. $(^-5)(^-100)(^-302) =$

19. $(1)(^-41)(^-6) =$

20. $(^-33)(213) =$

Integers

Dividing Integers

$$\frac{^-18}{^-3} = 6$$

Like signs = Positive

$$24 \div (^-4) = ^-6$$

Unlike signs = Negative

Solve each problem.

1. $100 \div (^-4) =$

2. $\frac{^-18}{18} =$

3. $^-60 \div 3 =$

4. $\frac{^-104}{8} =$

5. $120 \div (^-6) =$

6. $\frac{^-77}{7} =$

7. $88 \div (^-22) =$

8. $\frac{36}{^-9} =$

9. $^-188 \div 4 =$

10. $\frac{168}{21} =$

11. $144 \div (^-12) =$

12. $\frac{^-50}{^-5} =$

13. $80 \div (^-5) =$

14. $^-36 \div 6 =$

15. $72 \div 4 =$

16. $\frac{169}{^-13} =$

17. $\frac{210}{^-10} =$

18. $\frac{^-50}{^-5} =$

19. $^-150 \div 6 =$

20. $\frac{^-288}{^-12} =$

Integers

Dividing Integers

Solve each problem.

1. $^-14 \div 14 =$

2. $\dfrac{^-77}{11} =$

3. $60 \div (^-10) =$

4. $^-160 \div (^-40) =$

5. $^-72 \div 9 =$

6. $\dfrac{^-80}{10} =$

7. $\dfrac{^-755}{^-5} =$

8. $\dfrac{^-72}{8} =$

9. $^-54 \div (^-9) =$

10. $\dfrac{^-35}{^-7} =$

11. $^-195 \div (^-65) =$

12. $\dfrac{^-468}{26} =$

13. $^-150 \div (^-50) =$

14. $\dfrac{^-253}{11} =$

15. $189 \div (^-21) =$

16. $\dfrac{66}{^-2} =$

17. $75 \div (^-3) =$

18. $\dfrac{^-84}{^-7} =$

19. $^-210 \div (^-5) =$

20. $\dfrac{^-552}{^-23} =$

21. $^-94 \div 2 =$

22. $\dfrac{^-310}{5} =$

23. $^-125 \div 5 =$

24. $\dfrac{^-258}{^-3} =$

Integers

Mixed Practice with Integers

Solve each problem.

1. $(625 \div 5) \times 0.2 =$

2. $\dfrac{150}{(-5)} \times (-4) =$

3. $80 - (-22) =$

4. $\dfrac{-555}{(-5)} \times (-6) =$

5. $-3 \times 5 =$

6. $\dfrac{-424}{4} =$

7. $19 - 23 =$

8. $(\dfrac{-72}{9}) + (\dfrac{-64}{8}) + (\dfrac{44}{-11}) =$

9. $83 + (-85) =$

10. $(-34) + (-255) =$

11. $28 - (-65) =$

12. $28 - (-26) =$

13. $[-19 - (-21) - (-34)] \div (-6) =$

14. $[-18 - (-66) \, -22] \times 2 =$

15. $-61 - (-21) =$

16. $(16 - 21 + 34) \div (-8) =$

17. $-35 + 62 + (-80) =$

18. $[10 + (-31) + (-80)] \div 3 =$

19. $(-13 - 54 - 30) \times 2 =$

20. $[-160 + (-75) + 24] \times 4 =$

21. $56 \times 3 \times 21 =$

22. $(-12 + 13 + 55) \div 3 =$

Integers

Problem Solving with Integers

Solve each problem. Show your work.

1. A helicopter started out at an altitude of 0 feet. It then rose to an altitude of 2,150 feet. Then, it descended 400 feet in order to see a herd of bison. It then rose 4,200 feet in order to avoid a passing plane. After the plane passed, the helicopter descended 2,200 feet. What was the helicopter's altitude at the end?

2. Julio goes to school in a 9–story building. His first class of the day is on the second floor. For his second class, Julio goes up 5 floors. For his third class, Julio goes down 1 floor. For his fourth class, Julio goes up 3 floors, and for his last class he goes down 2 floors. What floor is Julio on during his last class?

3. Some number added to ⁻12 is 45. Add this number to 30. Multiply the answer by 3. What is the final number?

4. Some number multiplied by ⁻6 is 36. Multiply this number by 8. Divide the answer by 2. What is the final number?

5. A bus driver started her day with no passengers. Then, 13 people got on at the first stop. At the second stop, 8 people got on and 6 left the bus. At the third stop, 5 people got on and 3 left the bus. How many people are on the bus after the third stop?

6. The school library started the year with 9,561 books. At the end of the first week of school, 1,625 books had been checked out. At the end of the second week, 5,140 books had been checked out. By the end of two weeks 913 books had been returned. How many books were in the library at the end of the second week?

Real Numbers

Adding and Subtracting Real Numbers

$$^-4 + (^-3) + 2\frac{1}{3} = ^-7 + 2\frac{1}{3} = ^-6\frac{3}{3} + 2\frac{1}{3} = ^-4\frac{2}{3}$$

Solve each problem.

1. $^-3 + (^-3\frac{1}{4}) - (^-3\frac{3}{8}) =$

2. $^-5\frac{2}{3} - (^-6\frac{1}{5}) + 1\frac{7}{12} =$

3. $^-2 + 6\frac{1}{5} + (^-4\frac{1}{3}) =$

4. $^-6 - 2\frac{3}{5} + (^-7\frac{2}{5}) =$

5. $17.65 + (^-5\frac{1}{10}) + 13\frac{2}{5} =$

6. $7\frac{1}{7} - (^-9.33) + 7\frac{4}{7} =$

7. $5\frac{5}{12} + (^-6.44) - 14.69 =$

8. $7\frac{4}{13} + (^-9.21) - 16.32 =$

9. $^-1 + (^-2\frac{1}{3}) + (^-7\frac{3}{5}) =$

10. $13.23 - (^-31.73) =$

11. $2\frac{5}{7} - (^-5\frac{6}{9}) + \frac{1}{3} =$

12. $5\frac{5}{8} - (^-7\frac{2}{3}) - \frac{1}{9} =$

13. $4.38 + (^-4.38) =$

14. $7 + 13.3 + (^-9\frac{1}{6}) =$

15. $4\frac{1}{5} + (^-4.34) - 7\frac{1}{4} =$

16. $17 - 12.2 + (^-9\frac{2}{5}) =$

17. $12.26 - (^-7\frac{2}{5}) + 18\frac{1}{4} =$

18. $^-3\frac{2}{3} + (^-5\frac{5}{12}) =$

Real Numbers

Adding and Subtracting Real Numbers

Solve each problem.

1. $-8\frac{1}{2} + (-2\frac{4}{12}) - 8\frac{1}{3} =$

2. $5\frac{2}{5} + (-3.43) - 8\frac{3}{10} =$

3. $-6 - 7\frac{3}{4} + (-2\frac{2}{3}) =$

4. $-8 - 1\frac{3}{5} + (-6\frac{1}{8}) =$

5. $-2\frac{3}{7} + (-9\frac{6}{21}) - 5\frac{2}{3} =$

6. $3\frac{2}{5} + (-2.25) - 7\frac{2}{4} =$

7. $6\frac{1}{10} + (-3.25) - 12.65 =$

8. $-11.08 - (-12.67) =$

9. $-2 - (-3\frac{1}{8}) + (-4\frac{3}{4}) =$

10. $17 - 12.2 - (-8\frac{4}{9}) =$

11. $6\frac{2}{3} - (-1\frac{2}{3}) + \frac{2}{3} =$

12. $3\frac{1}{2} - (-6\frac{1}{3}) - \frac{3}{5} =$

13. $12 - 15.3 + (-7\frac{2}{3}) =$

14. $-5 - (-7\frac{3}{7}) + (-2\frac{5}{8}) =$

15. $3\frac{1}{15} + (-4.38) - 13.47 =$

16. $-5.23 + 3.33 =$

17. $14.33 - (-5\frac{3}{4}) + 13\frac{2}{3} =$

18. $17\frac{8}{9} - 12.2 + 16\frac{2}{7} =$

19. $5\frac{2}{3} - (-5.61) - 8\frac{1}{5} =$

20. $11.62 + (-8\frac{6}{7}) - \frac{18}{9} =$

21. $3\frac{7}{10} + (-4.23) - 7\frac{3}{8} =$

22. $11\frac{2}{5} - 17.8 + 13\frac{4}{5} =$

Real Numbers

Multiplying and Dividing Real Numbers

$$2 \times 3 \times \frac{1}{2} = 6 \times \frac{1}{2} = \frac{6}{1} \times \frac{1}{2} = 3$$

$$2\frac{1}{2} \times 1\frac{3}{4} \div 1\frac{1}{2} = \frac{5}{2} \times \frac{7}{4} \div \frac{3}{2} = \frac{5}{2} \times \frac{7}{4} \times \frac{2}{3} = \frac{35}{12} = 2\frac{11}{12}$$

Solve each problem.

1. $2\frac{1}{3} \div 1\frac{1}{2} \times \frac{5}{6} =$

2. $2\frac{1}{7} \div (^-5.56) =$

3. $^-3 \times 2\frac{1}{5} \times (^-7\frac{1}{3}) =$

4. $7 \div 2.5 \times (^-3\frac{2}{5}) =$

5. $^-8\frac{2}{3} \times 3\frac{7}{15} =$

6. $5\frac{1}{3} \times 9.80 \times 0 =$

7. $1\frac{5}{12} \times 3.29 =$

8. $11 \times 3\frac{1}{12} \times (^-3) =$

9. $7 \times (^-2\frac{1}{3}) \times 2 =$

10. $(^-3\frac{1}{4})(^-3\frac{1}{4}) \div 2 =$

11. $5\frac{1}{2} \div (^-3\frac{1}{6}) =$

12. $2\frac{2}{3} \times (^-6\frac{1}{5}) =$

13. $^-6.3 \times 2 \times \frac{1}{2} =$

14. $10 \div 12.1 \div (^-6\frac{1}{6}) =$

15. $9.21 \times (^-7\frac{1}{3}) \div 25\frac{5}{9} =$

16. $6.21 \times (^-1.37) =$

17. $10.6 \div (^-2\frac{1}{2}) \times 3\frac{1}{4} =$

18. $3.6 \times (^-31.72) =$

Real Numbers

Multiplying and Dividing Real Numbers

Solve each problem.

1. $6\frac{1}{5} \times 3.55 \times 0 =$

2. $5\frac{1}{3} \div (^-3.84) =$

3. $^-6 \times 8\frac{2}{8} \times (^-1\frac{1}{4}) =$

4. $13 \times 5\frac{1}{10} \times (^-2) =$

5. $^-5\frac{1}{6} \times 2\frac{7}{18} =$

6. $1\frac{1}{14} \div (^-3\frac{2}{7}) =$

7. $3\frac{3}{8} \times 2.27 =$

8. $^-2.2 \times 5 \times \frac{1}{7} =$

9. $2 \times (^-1\frac{1}{2}) \times 6 =$

10. $10 \div 2.5 \times (^-4\frac{4}{7}) =$

11. $5.25 \times (^-3.89) =$

12. $2\frac{1}{5} \div 6\frac{3}{7} \div \frac{4}{6} =$

13. $(^-7\frac{2}{8})(^-3\frac{2}{8}) \div 0.2 =$

14. $8.10 \times (^-5\frac{1}{6}) \div 15\frac{5}{6} =$

15. $4.2 \times (^-12.12) =$

16. $3\frac{2}{3} \div (^-6\frac{1}{5}) =$

17. $12.2 \times (^-6\frac{1}{5}) \times 3\frac{2}{5} =$

18. $12.12 \times (^-12\frac{2}{6}) \div 12\frac{1}{3} =$

19. $13.5 \div (^-3\frac{2}{3}) \times 6\frac{3}{7} =$

20. $12 \times 12.3 \times (^-6\frac{1}{2}) =$

21. $12.8 \times (^-5\frac{2}{3}) \times 2\frac{4}{5} =$

22. $13.26 \times (^-8\frac{1}{3}) \div 12\frac{5}{7} =$

 CD-104315 • © Carson-Dellosa

Real Numbers

Order of Operations with Real Numbers

$$^-4 \times 2 + 2 = ^-8 + 2 = ^-6$$

$$2\frac{1}{4} \div (4 + 8) = \frac{9}{8} \div 12 = \frac{9}{8} \times \frac{1}{12} = \frac{9}{96} \text{ or } \frac{3}{32}$$

Solve each problem. Use the order of operations rules.

1. $2 \times 3\ [7 + (6 \div 2)] =$

2. $\frac{2}{3}(^-15 - 4) =$

3. $^-8 \div (^-2) + 5 \times (\frac{^-1}{2}) - 25 \div 5 =$

4. $^-30 \div 6 + 4\frac{1}{5} =$

5. $(9\frac{1}{3} + 4\frac{1}{3}) \div 6 - (^-12) =$

6. $\dfrac{[(60 \div 4) + 35]}{(^-12 + 35)} =$

7. $\frac{3}{4}\ [(^-15 + 4) + (6 + 7) \div (^-3)] =$

8. $3[^-3(2 - 8) - 6] =$

Real Numbers

Order of Operations with Real Numbers

Solve each problem. Use the order of operations rules.

1. $3 \times 3[2 - (9 \div 3)] =$

2. $\frac{1}{2}(^-12 + 6) =$

3. $(5\frac{1}{5} - 6\frac{1}{5}) \times 6 - (^-16) =$

4. $^-20 \div 3 + 2\frac{2}{3} =$

5. $^-5 \div (^-3) - 2 \times (^-\frac{1}{3}) - 21 \div 7 =$

6. $\dfrac{[(20 \div 2) + 10]}{(^-10 + 20 + 30)} =$

7. $2[^-5(4 - 12) - 3] =$

8. $\frac{1}{2}[(^-12 - 2) + (1 + 8) \div (^-8)] =$

9. $[(3 \times 3) - (30 \div 6)] + (^-27) - 13 =$

10. $2 \div [(4 \div 2) + (32 \div 8)] =$

11. $30 \times [(3 \times 9) - (21 \div 7)] + (^-32) =$

Real Numbers

Comparing Real Numbers

$3.55 \bigcirc 4.25$ $4\frac{1}{2} \bigcirc 4.25$

$3.55 < 4.25$ $4.50 > 4.25$

Use <, >, or = to make each statement true.

1. $1.5 \bigcirc 1\frac{2}{3}$

2. $^-0.4 \bigcirc ^-0.\overline{4}$

3. $1.088 \bigcirc 1.88$

4. $1{,}983.45 \bigcirc 7{,}551.7$

5. $13.26 \bigcirc 132.6$

6. $12\frac{5}{8} \bigcirc 12.6$

7. $232.33 \bigcirc 23.233$

8. $2.5 \bigcirc 2\frac{1}{2}$

9. $^-9\frac{36}{48} \bigcirc ^-9.77$

10. $4.25 \bigcirc 4\frac{1}{4}$

Order the decimals and fractions in each series from least to greatest.

$2\frac{1}{2}, 2\frac{2}{5}, 2.3$ $2.3, 2\frac{2}{5}, 2\frac{1}{2}$

11. $^-6\frac{1}{5}, ^-6.66, ^-6\frac{4}{5}$

12. $5\frac{2}{3}, 5.45, 5\frac{3}{5}$

13. $^-4\frac{1}{5}, ^-4\frac{2}{3}, ^-4\frac{5}{7}$

14. $3.15, 3.8, 3\frac{2}{5}$

15. $^-2\frac{1}{4}, 2\frac{7}{8}, 2\frac{3}{9}$

16. $^-1\frac{4}{5}, ^-1\frac{9}{10}, ^-1\frac{7}{8}$

17. $2.51, 2.511, 2.5111$

18. $10.76, 10.761, 10.770$

19. $4\frac{2}{3}, ^-4\frac{6}{9}, 4.34$

20. $5\frac{1}{2}, 5\frac{1}{3}, 5\frac{3}{4}$

Equations

Open Sentences

$$\frac{1}{2} \times 10 = q \qquad\qquad \frac{49}{7} - 10 = a$$

$$\frac{1}{2} \times \frac{10}{1} = q \qquad\qquad 7 - 10 = a$$

$$5 = q \qquad\qquad {}^-3 = a$$

Solve each equation for the variable.

1. ${}^-4 \times 5 - 9 = d$

2. $1 + 2.78 - 7.5 = z$

3. $(11 + 3)\, 7 = j$

4. $-\frac{3}{5} \div \frac{1}{15} + \left({}^-3\frac{1}{3}\right) = y$

5. $\dfrac{[2 + ({}^-18)]}{4} = p$

6. $\left[\dfrac{(6 - 12)}{3}\right] + 4 = p$

7. $\frac{1}{5} \times ({}^-12) + ({}^-9) = w$

8. $2\frac{3}{5} \div \frac{15}{45} = f$

9. ${}^-7.5 \times 3.3 + 13 = g$

10. $3.34 + 2.22 \div 3 = q$

11. $\frac{2}{6} \times 13 - 6 = m$

12. $\dfrac{[15 + ({}^-7)]}{2} = r$

13. $5 \times 3.61 - 16.8 = n$

14. $\left[\dfrac{({}^-35 + 12)}{3}\right] + 7 = b$

Equations

Open Sentences

$20 = y \times 2$, if $y = 10$
$20 = 10 \times 2$
$20 = 20$ True

Evaluate each expression as true or false for the given value of the variable.

1. $^-t \times 5 - 6 = ^-23$, if $t = 5$

2. $[\dfrac{(18 + 11)}{b}] + 6 = 13$, if $b = 3$

3. $2 + y = 9$, if $y = 6$

4. $r + 6.32 \div 3 = 2.2$, if $r = ^-3$

5. $(\dfrac{m}{6}) + (^-4) = 0$, if $m = 6$

6. $z + 13 \div 6.5 = 5$, if $z = ^-5$

7. $y(6 + 3) + 2 = 236$, if $y = 26$

8. $\dfrac{2}{6} \times 13 - k = 7$, if $k = 6$

9. $11.2 + 0.2 - r = 8.2$, if $r = 3.2$

10. $f(2 + 3) + 1 = 22$, if $f = 16$

11. $3x + 14 = 17$, if $x = ^-1$

12. $6 + x = 3\dfrac{1}{3}$, if $x = ^-3\dfrac{1}{2}$

13. $^-\dfrac{2}{5} \div \dfrac{1}{15} + (\dfrac{1}{3} \times c) = ^-5\dfrac{1}{3}$, if $c = 2$

14. $7 + (e - 30) = ^-12$, if $e = ^-13$

Equations

Evaluating Expressions

> If $w = \frac{1}{5}$, $x = 4$, and $y = -5$,
>
> then $3x(5w + 2y) = 3 \cdot 4[5(\frac{1}{5}) + 2(-5)] = 12(1 - 10) = 12(-9) = -108$

Evaluate each expression if $w = \frac{1}{5}$, $x = 4$, and $y = -5$.

1. $y(w + 7) =$

2. $3w + 4(x - y) =$

3. $6[w + (-y)] =$

4. $wx + x + 6xy =$

5. $5(w - 2y) =$

6. $w(x + y) =$

7. $w(xw + xy) =$

8. $7w - (xy + 3) =$

9. $3w(3y + 5x) =$

10. $wx(3w + 3y - 6) =$

11. $3w - 4x =$

12. $10y(4y + 2w) =$

13. $8x + (-12x) =$

14. $4w - 7x + 3y - 2w =$

Equations

Simplifying Expressions

$$2(x + 3y) = 2x + 2 \cdot 3y = 2x + 6y$$

Expand each expression using the distributive property.

1. $4(2r + 6y) =$

2. $2(3p - 3p) =$

3. $^-6(2b + 3c) =$

4. $7(^-c + 6d) =$

5. $2(x - 12) =$

6. $12(2y + 5w) =$

7. $3(2 + r) =$

8. $3(w - 4) =$

9. $8[y + (^-2x)] =$

10. $5(2 + 13y) =$

11. $2k[^-xy + (^-8)] =$

12. $^-7(2x + 9) =$

13. $5(2y + 5x) =$

14. $3(x + 2y + z) =$

Equations

Simplifying Expressions

$$2(3w + 2b) = 6w + 2 \cdot 2b = 6w + 4b$$

Expand each expression using the distributive property.

1. $^-5(2s + 2m) =$

2. $4(2d + 6b) =$

3. $^-4(j + k + g) =$

4. $2(^-t + 4e) =$

5. $7(3y - 8) =$

6. $6(2g + y) =$

7. $4(3 + k) =$

8. $6(3v + 5c) =$

9. $2(t - 6q) =$

10. $^-5(3w + 5e) =$

11. $^-5[7h + (^-3p)] =$

12. $^-3(8g + 13a) =$

13. $3(10e + 3f) =$

14. $3d(^-nm + 7) =$

Equations

Simplifying Expressions

$$4a - 3a + 7z = (4 - 3)a + 7z = a + 7z$$

Combine like terms.

1. $3x + 3y + xy - 6xy + 5x + (^-4y) =$

2. $12p + 4pd - 2p + 6pd =$

3. $2x + 3xy + 4x + 5xy + 6x=$

4. $4x - 2x + 6xy + 21x + (^-9xy) - 9 =$

5. $^-3n + 12 - 4n =$

6. $5e + 6ed + 5d - 7ed + 7 =$

7. $3xy + 13xy - 12xy =$

8. $2r + 4ry - 5r + 3x - 4ry =$

9. $10ax - 2ax + 12x - 2a + (^-2x) =$

10. $7a + a - 2a + 3ab - ab + 2ab =$

11. $7r + 2r - 4 =$

12. $5m + 2m + 40m + m + 17 =$

13. $23x - 7x + 4x =$

14. $4x + 3y - 3xy + 6x - 2xy =$

Equations

Simplifying Expressions

$$5g - 3g + 2h = (5 - 3)g + 2h = 2g + 2h$$

Combine like terms.

1. $7(2x + 5y) + 6xy - 6(3xy + 5x) =$

2. $10p + 5pd - 2p + 6pd =$

3. $9x - 4x + 2x + 8(6x + 2x) =$

4. $3(x - 5x) + 2(xy + 7x) + (^-7xy) =$

5. $3c - 4bc + (^-7b) + 3[2bc - (^-b)] =$

6. $^-2a - [^-3(a + 7)] - 4(^-a + b) =$

7. $2t + 12t - 4(n + 4n) =$

8. $6r + 5r - 8p + 6p + 7(2r - 4r) =$

9. $3n(x^- y) + 3n(x + y) - 2 =$

10. $3[h - (^-k)] + 2[^-3h + (^-4k)] =$

11. $^-2(g + 5g) + ^-2[6f - (^-12g)] =$

12. $4(2x + 2y) - 2[3xy - (^-5x)] =$

13. $5m + 3mn - (^-9n) + 2(m - n) =$

14. $5xy - 12xy + 12xy - 9(x + y) =$

Equations

Solving Addition Equations

$$1.4 = {}^-2.4 + x$$
$$1.4 + 2.4 = {}^-2.4 + 2.4 + x$$
$$3.8 = 0 + x$$
$$3.8 = x$$

Solve each equation for the variable.

1. $x + ({}^-5\frac{3}{4}) = {}^-10\frac{1}{4}$

2. ${}^-35 = x + 35$

3. $w + 79 = {}^-95$

4. ${}^-\frac{1}{4} + x = {}^-\frac{1}{4}$

5. $7 + c = {}^-14$

6. ${}^-4.5 = 9\frac{1}{2} + c$

7. ${}^-21 = t + 18$

8. $22 = c + ({}^-13)$

9. ${}^-9 + r = 22$

10. $x + ({}^-8) = 9$

11. $3.5 = n + 4.6$

12. ${}^-2\frac{1}{2} + k = {}^-3\frac{5}{7}$

13. ${}^-2,929 + t = 4,242$

14. $z + 5.2 = 7.1$

Equations

Solving Subtraction Equations

$$32 = x - (^-8)$$
$$32 = x + 8$$
$$32 - 8 = x + 8 - 8$$
$$24 = x + 0$$
$$24 = x$$

Solve each equation for the variable.

1. $^-2{,}547 = n - 5{,}534$

2. $^-44 = m - 32$

3. $t - (^-8) = 45$

4. $-\dfrac{1}{3} - g = -\dfrac{1}{3}$

5. $^-15 = p - 6$

6. $3.65 = n - 7$

7. $34 = b - (^-2)$

8. $a + (^-4\dfrac{1}{3}) = ^-15\dfrac{1}{3}$

9. $f - 16 = ^-32$

10. $x - 8 = 34$

11. $^-3.4 = h - 8.5$

12. $^-2.2 = 8\dfrac{4}{5} + d$

13. $^-3\dfrac{2}{3} + k = ^-6\dfrac{3}{4}$

14. $z - (^-21.5) = ^-2.356$

CD-104315 • © Carson-Dellosa

Equations

Solving Addition and Subtraction Equations

$$10 = c - 8$$
$$10 + 8 = c - 8 + 8$$
$$18 = c + 0$$
$$18 = c$$

Solve each equation for the variable.

1. $-\dfrac{3}{4} + j = {}^-3\dfrac{1}{2}$

2. $11.4 - k = 5.2$

3. $-8\dfrac{3}{7} + t = {}^-9\dfrac{2}{5}$

4. $^-3.1 = 4\dfrac{3}{4} + e$

5. $b + ({}^-9) = 36$

6. $5.77 = q + 9$

7. $^-56 = c - ({}^-8)$

8. $^-3,282 = n + 1,111$

9. $t + 12 = {}^-18$

10. $^-6.7 = y - 27$

11. $f + ({}^-3\dfrac{1}{4}) = {}^-7\dfrac{1}{4}$

12. $w - ({}^-43.7) = {}^-3.674$

13. $31 = u - 12$

14. $x + 9 = {}^-22$

Equations

Solving Multiplication Equations

$$4y = {}^-24$$
$$4y \div 4 = {}^-24 \div 4$$
$$1y = {}^-6$$
$$y = {}^-6$$

Solve each equation for the variable.

1. $36 = {}^-6t$

2. $3m = {}^-5$

3. ${}^-169 = 13b$

4. $0.24t = 1.2$

5. ${}^-15m = 15$

6. $43\frac{1}{2} = {}^-13d$

7. ${}^-7b = {}^-77$

8. ${}^-12n = {}^-56$

9. $3.5 = 7x$

10. ${}^-0.0006 = 0.02c$

11. ${}^-2.1 = 0.7c$

12. $33k = {}^-878$

13. $1\frac{2}{3} = 9x$

14. $1.44 = 12r$

Equations

Solving Multiplication Equations

$$2y = {}^-12$$
$$2y \div 2 = {}^-12 \div 2$$
$$1y = {}^-6$$
$$y = {}^-6$$

Solve each equation for the variable.

1. ${}^-250 = 25s$

2. $18\frac{1}{3} = {}^-12w$

3. $72 = {}^-8r$

4. $15n = {}^-3$

5. ${}^-12q = 12$

6. ${}^-0.0009 = 0.03q$

7. $56 = {}^-7e$

8. $43u = {}^-734$

9. ${}^-4.5 = 9h$

10. $0.48y = 2.4$

11. ${}^-6.7 = {}^-0.137k$

12. $9h = {}^-90$

13. $2\frac{4}{6} = 5e$

14. ${}^-13g = {}^-78$

Equations

Solving Division Equations

$$\frac{x}{2} = 6$$
$$2 \cdot \frac{x}{2} = 6 \cdot 2$$
$$x = 12$$

Solve each equation for the variable.

1. $\frac{m}{7} = 42$

2. $^-12 = \frac{t}{4}$

3. $0.9 = \frac{k}{81}$

4. $(\frac{1}{7})n = ^-28$

5. $(\frac{3}{4})z = 144$

6. $\frac{r}{17} = ^-23$

7. $\frac{u}{4} = ^-36$

8. $^-3 = (\frac{1}{3})x$

9. $^-15 = \frac{x}{3}$

10. $\frac{x}{7} = 56$

11. $(\frac{1}{12})c = 0.6$

12. $(\frac{3}{7})h = 4.5$

13. $\frac{x}{4.1} = 18$

14. $(\frac{1}{4})c = ^-8$

Equations

Solving Multiplication and Division Equations

$$2y = {}^-12 \qquad\qquad \frac{n}{2} = 8$$
$$2y \div 2 = {}^-12 \div 2 \qquad 2 \cdot \frac{n}{2} = 8 \cdot 2$$
$$1y = {}^-6 \qquad\qquad n = 16$$
$$y = {}^-6$$

Solve each equation for the variable.

1. $6n = {}^-72$

2. $^-77 = \frac{t}{11}$

3. $12a = 156$

4. $\frac{f}{3.6} = 16$

5. $(\frac{1}{5})m = 22$

6. $^-12r = 12$

7. $54 = {}^-9u$

8. $^-6 = \frac{x}{6}$

9. $(\frac{2}{3})c = 5.9$

10. $\frac{h}{9} = 63$

11. $3.7 = {}^-0.21w$

12. $4.5 = 9y$

13. $(2\frac{3}{5})a = 6$

14. $(\frac{5}{12})b = {}^-12$

Equations

Solving Equations with Two Operations

$$2y - 10 = 30$$
$$2y - 10 + 10 = 30 + 10$$
$$\frac{2y}{2} = \frac{40}{2}$$
$$y = 20$$

Solve each equation for the variable. Write the answer in simplest form.

1. $14 = 6c - 4$

2. $13n - 13 = {}^-12$

3. $5x - 5 = {}^-10$

4. $23x - 12 = {}^-33$

5. $10 = 3y + 5$

6. ${}^-42 = 6b + 8$

7. ${}^-23 = 3e - ({}^-9)$

8. $16 + 4y = {}^-32$

9. ${}^-8r - 9 = {}^-24$

10. $16 + \frac{r}{2} = {}^-11$

11. $12 = 3y - 12$

12. $2x - 5 = 16$

13. $\frac{3y}{4} = 12$

14. $16 = {}^-2v + 9$

Equations

Solving Equations Using the Distributive Property

$$2(a - 3) = 14$$
$$2a - 6 = 14$$
$$2a - 6 + 6 = 14 + 6$$
$$\frac{2a}{2} = \frac{20}{2}$$
$$a = 10$$

Solve each equation for the variable.

1. $^{-}4(6 + n) + 3 = 36$

2. $3(8 - 6n) = 42$

3. $35 = {}^{-}7(z + 8)$

4. $2(n + 6) = 80$

5. $30 = 5[(\frac{r}{5}){}^{-}3]$

6. $^{-}23 = 5(t - 4)$

7. $^{-}7(t - 7) = {}^{-}14$

8. $2(9x - 8) = {}^{-}22$

9. $16(x - 3) = {}^{-}33$

10. $^{-}36 = 2(x + 4)$

11. $8(2x - 4) + 4 = 24$

12. $3(c + 4) = {}^{-}8$

13. $5(3 - \frac{c}{7}) = 8$

14. $36 = 6(x - 5)$

Problem Solving

Writing Algebraic Expressions

Three times a number increased by 5 $3x + 5$
A number increased by 3 $x + 3$
A number divided by 2 $x \div 2$ or $\frac{x}{2}$
The product of 2 and 6 $2 \cdot 6$

Write the algebraic expression.

1. Two-fifths of a number decreased by 3

2. Twelve times a number decreased by 4

3. Eight times the difference between x and 7

4. The product of 3 and a number increased by 6

5. One-third times a number increased by 7

6. Four increased by 7 times a number

7. Seven times the sum of twice a number and 16

8. Eleven times the sum of a number and 5 times the number

9. Five times a number plus 6 times the number

10. The quotient of a number and 5 decreased by 3

11. Four times the sum of a number and 8

12. A number increased by 9 times the number

Name _____ Date _____

Problem Solving

Writing Algebraic Expressions

Two times a number increased by 4	$2x + 4$
A number increased by 2	$x + 2$
A number divided by 4	$x \div 4$ or $\frac{x}{4}$
The product of 3 and 5	$3 \cdot 5$

Write an equation for each expression.

1. Two-thirds of a number increased by 9

2. The quotient of 6 and a number increased by 3

3. Nine more than the quotient of b and 4

4. Four-sevenths of a number minus 6

5. Three-fourths times a number increased by 6

6. Three increased by 4 times a number

7. Three times a number plus 7 times the number

8. A number increased by 9 times the number

9. Three times a number increased by 9

10. The quotient of a number and 4 increased by 2

11. Six times the difference between c and 7

12. Two times the sum of a number and 11

Problem Solving

Writing Algebraic Expressions

Eight more than a number is 28. Find the number.
$$8 + x = 28$$
$$8 - 8 + x = 28 - 8$$
$$x = 20$$

Write an equation for each expression and solve.

1. The cost of 1 saddle is $220.00. What is the cost of 7 saddles?

2. One–third of a number is $^-15$. Find the number.

3. The cost of 6 cakes is $48.00. What is the cost of each cake?

4. Four times a number is 52. Find the number.

5. The product of $^-9$ and a number is 36. Find the number.

6. Three times a number is 24. Find the number.

7. A number increased by 8 is $^-24$. Find the number.

Problem Solving

Writing Algebraic Expressions

A number decreased by 7 is 10. Find the number.
$$x - 7 = 10$$
$$x - 7 + 7 = 10 + 7$$
$$x = 17$$

Write an equation for each expression and solve.

1. Three times a number is 63. Find the number.

2. The product of $^-4$ and a number is 28. Find the number.

3. One–fourth of a number is 13. Find the number.

4. Four times a number is 24. Find the number.

5. The cost of 6 boxes of cookies is $30.00. What is the cost of each box?

6. The cost of a television is $234.00. What is the cost of 3 televisions?

7. A number increased by 10 is 54. Find the number.

Problem Solving

Writing Algebraic Expressions

Five more than 2 times a number is 21. What is the number?

$$5 + 2x = 21$$
$$5 - 5 + 2x = 21 - 5$$
$$2x = 16$$
$$x = 8$$

Write an equation for each expression and solve.

1. Two times the sum of a number and 5 is 26. What is the number?

2. The quotient of a number and 3 decreased by 6 is 7. What is the number?

3. The product of a number and 4 increased by 7 is 5. What is the number?

4. Three more than 5 times a number is 58. What is the number?

5. Six more than a number is ⁻31. What is the number?

6. Two–thirds of a number increased by 3 is 11. What is the number?

7. Ten less than 2 times a number is 24. What is the number?

Problem Solving

Writing Algebraic Expressions

> One number plus 4 times that number = 125. Find the number.
> $$x + 4x = 125$$
> $$5x = 125$$
> $$x = 25$$

Write an equation for each expression and solve.

1. One number plus 7 times that number equals 160. Find the number.

2. One number plus 4 times that number is 55. Find the number.

3. One number is 8 times a second number. Four times the smaller number plus twice the larger number equals 68. Find the number.

4. The sum of 2 numbers is 126. The larger number is 5 times larger than the smaller number. Find the number.

5. The sum of 2 numbers is 54. The larger number is twice the smaller number. Find the number.

6. The difference between 2 numbers is 48. The first number is 5 times the second number. Find the number.

7. There were 606 tickets sold for the school lacrosse game. Students bought 5 times as many tickets as the faculty did. Find the number of student and faculty tickets sold.

Problem Solving

Writing Algebraic Expressions

Eight times a number equals 18 less than 2 times the number. Find the number.

$$8x = 2x - 18$$
$$8x - 2x = 2x - 2x - 18$$
$$6x = {}^-18$$
$$x = {}^-3$$

Write an equation for each expression and solve.

1. One half of a number is 14 more than 2 times the number. Find the number.

2. Forty increased by 4 times a number is 8 less than 6 times the number. Find the number.

3. Nineteen increased by 3 times a number is 4 less than 4 times the number. Find the number.

4. Four times the sum of a number and 3 is 7 times the number decreased by 3. Find the number.

5. Twice a number decreased by 44 is 6 times the sum of the number and 3 times the number. Find the number.

6. Thirty decreased by 3 times a number is 6 less than 3 times the number. Find the number.

7. Twelve increased by 6 times a number is 6 less than 7 times the number. Find the number.

Inequalities

Number Lines

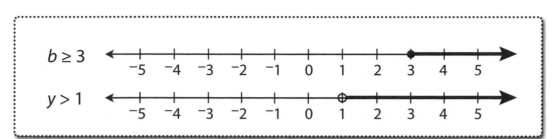

Graph each inequality on the number line.

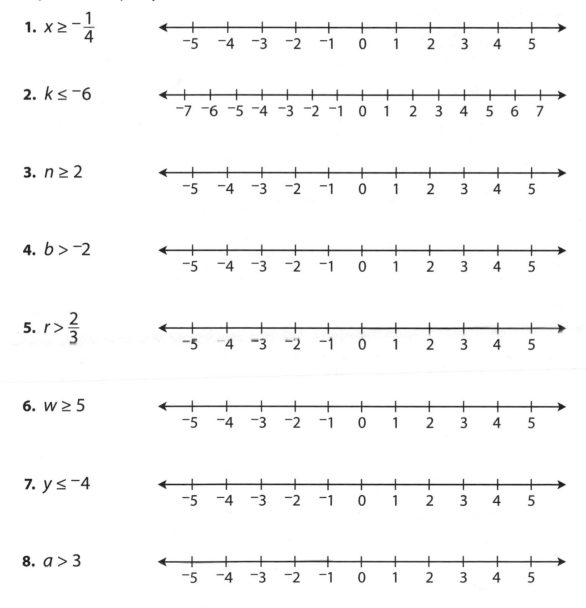

1. $x \geq -\dfrac{1}{4}$

2. $k \leq {}^-6$

3. $n \geq 2$

4. $b > {}^-2$

5. $r > \dfrac{2}{3}$

6. $w \geq 5$

7. $y \leq {}^-4$

8. $a > 3$

Inequalities

Solving Inequalities with Addition and Subtraction

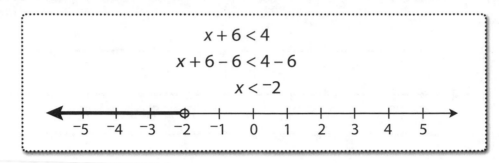

$$x + 6 < 4$$
$$x + 6 - 6 < 4 - 6$$
$$x < {}^-2$$

Solve each inequality and graph the answer on the number line.

1. $2.3 \geq s + 3$

2. $6 > y + 2$

3. $7 + n \leq 9$

4. $d + \dfrac{2}{3} \geq \dfrac{1}{3}$

5. $f - 4 > -2$

6. $x - 3 \leq 2$

7. $1 > d - 3$

8. $-2 \leq 2 + g$

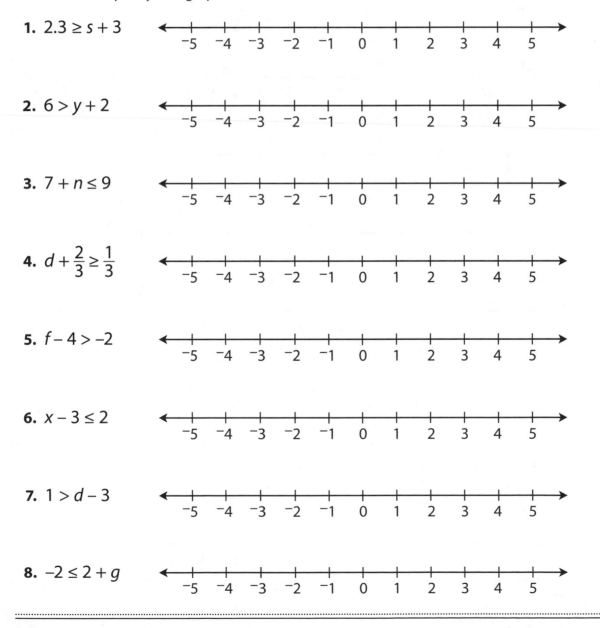

Inequalities

Solving Inequalities with Multiplication and Division

$$(-\tfrac{1}{2})x \geq 2$$

$$-\tfrac{2}{1} \cdot (-\tfrac{1}{2})x \geq 2(-\tfrac{2}{1})$$

$$x \leq {}^-4$$

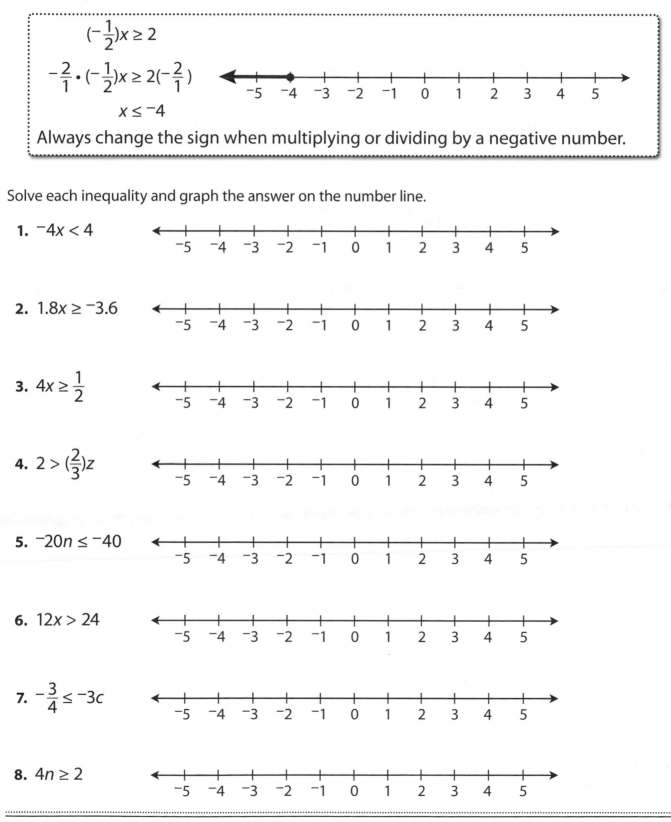

Always change the sign when multiplying or dividing by a negative number.

Solve each inequality and graph the answer on the number line.

1. $^-4x < 4$

2. $1.8x \geq {}^-3.6$

3. $4x \geq \tfrac{1}{2}$

4. $2 > (\tfrac{2}{3})z$

5. $^-20n \leq {}^-40$

6. $12x > 24$

7. $-\tfrac{3}{4} \leq {}^-3c$

8. $4n \geq 2$

Inequalities

Solving Inequalities

Solve each inequality and graph the answer on the number line.

1. $r \geq 3$

2. $x > {}^-2$

3. ${}^-r \leq 1$

4. $x \geq 3$

5. $t \leq {}^-4$

6. $2c \geq 2$

7. ${}^-4 \geq 2b$

8. $m \geq {}^-4$

9. $e + 1 \leq 3$

10. $5t \geq {}^-5$

Inequalities

Solving Inequalities

Solve each inequality and graph the answer on the number line.

1. $c + 1 > {}^-4$

$$\longleftrightarrow\!\!|\!\!|\!\!|\!\!|\!\!|\!\!|\!\!|\!\!|\!\!|\!\!|\!\!|\!\!|\!\!|\!\!|\!\!|\!\!|\!\!|\!\!|\!\!|\!\!|\!\!\longrightarrow$$
$$^-10\ ^-9\ ^-8\ ^-7\ ^-6\ ^-5\ ^-4\ ^-3\ ^-2\ ^-1\ 0\ 1\ 2\ 3\ 4\ 5\ 6\ 7\ 8\ 9\ 10$$

2. $6.5c < 6.5$

$$^-10\ ^-9\ ^-8\ ^-7\ ^-6\ ^-5\ ^-4\ ^-3\ ^-2\ ^-1\ 0\ 1\ 2\ 3\ 4\ 5\ 6\ 7\ 8\ 9\ 10$$

3. $^-4 \geq s - (^-2)$

$$^-10\ ^-9\ ^-8\ ^-7\ ^-6\ ^-5\ ^-4\ ^-3\ ^-2\ ^-1\ 0\ 1\ 2\ 3\ 4\ 5\ 6\ 7\ 8\ 9\ 10$$

4. $(\frac{1}{2})y > {}^-5$

$$^-10\ ^-9\ ^-8\ ^-7\ ^-6\ ^-5\ ^-4\ ^-3\ ^-2\ ^-1\ 0\ 1\ 2\ 3\ 4\ 5\ 6\ 7\ 8\ 9\ 10$$

5. $d - 4.5 \geq {}^-1.5$

$$^-10\ ^-9\ ^-8\ ^-7\ ^-6\ ^-5\ ^-4\ ^-3\ ^-2\ ^-1\ 0\ 1\ 2\ 3\ 4\ 5\ 6\ 7\ 8\ 9\ 10$$

6. $^-14.5 \leq x + {}^-21.5$

$$^-10\ ^-9\ ^-8\ ^-7\ ^-6\ ^-5\ ^-4\ ^-3\ ^-2\ ^-1\ 0\ 1\ 2\ 3\ 4\ 5\ 6\ 7\ 8\ 9\ 10$$

7. $^-13 < g - 12$

$$^-10\ ^-9\ ^-8\ ^-7\ ^-6\ ^-5\ ^-4\ ^-3\ ^-2\ ^-1\ 0\ 1\ 2\ 3\ 4\ 5\ 6\ 7\ 8\ 9\ 10$$

8. $h + 9 > 12$

$$^-10\ ^-9\ ^-8\ ^-7\ ^-6\ ^-5\ ^-4\ ^-3\ ^-2\ ^-1\ 0\ 1\ 2\ 3\ 4\ 5\ 6\ 7\ 8\ 9\ 10$$

9. $-\frac{n}{3} \geq 2$

$$^-10\ ^-9\ ^-8\ ^-7\ ^-6\ ^-5\ ^-4\ ^-3\ ^-2\ ^-1\ 0\ 1\ 2\ 3\ 4\ 5\ 6\ 7\ 8\ 9\ 10$$

10. $10 > r + 14$

$$^-10\ ^-9\ ^-8\ ^-7\ ^-6\ ^-5\ ^-4\ ^-3\ ^-2\ ^-1\ 0\ 1\ 2\ 3\ 4\ 5\ 6\ 7\ 8\ 9\ 10$$

Inequalities

Solving Inequalities

$$^-20x + 8 > 4x - 40$$
$$^-20x + 20x + 8 > 4x + 20x - 40$$
$$8 > 24x - 40$$
$$48 > 24x$$
$$2 > x$$

Solve each inequality and graph the answer on the number line.

1. $^-6\frac{1}{3} \geq k + \frac{2}{3}$

$\xleftarrow{\hspace{0.3cm}}$ $^-10$ $^-9$ $^-8$ $^-7$ $^-6$ $^-5$ $^-4$ $^-3$ $^-2$ $^-1$ 0 1 2 3 4 5 6 7 8 9 10 $\xrightarrow{\hspace{0.3cm}}$

2. $h - 3 \leq 2$

$\xleftarrow{\hspace{0.3cm}}$ $^-10$ $^-9$ $^-8$ $^-7$ $^-6$ $^-5$ $^-4$ $^-3$ $^-2$ $^-1$ 0 1 2 3 4 5 6 7 8 9 10 $\xrightarrow{\hspace{0.3cm}}$

3. $a - 2.07 \geq 3.93$

$\xleftarrow{\hspace{0.3cm}}$ $^-10$ $^-9$ $^-8$ $^-7$ $^-6$ $^-5$ $^-4$ $^-3$ $^-2$ $^-1$ 0 1 2 3 4 5 6 7 8 9 10 $\xrightarrow{\hspace{0.3cm}}$

4. $1.3q \geq 8.7$

$\xleftarrow{\hspace{0.3cm}}$ $^-10$ $^-9$ $^-8$ $^-7$ $^-6$ $^-5$ $^-4$ $^-3$ $^-2$ $^-1$ 0 1 2 3 4 5 6 7 8 9 10 $\xrightarrow{\hspace{0.3cm}}$

5. $^-11 < k + {^-13}$

$\xleftarrow{\hspace{0.3cm}}$ $^-10$ $^-9$ $^-8$ $^-7$ $^-6$ $^-5$ $^-4$ $^-3$ $^-2$ $^-1$ 0 1 2 3 4 5 6 7 8 9 10 $\xrightarrow{\hspace{0.3cm}}$

6. $^-14 \geq h - 8$

$\xleftarrow{\hspace{0.3cm}}$ $^-10$ $^-9$ $^-8$ $^-7$ $^-6$ $^-5$ $^-4$ $^-3$ $^-2$ $^-1$ 0 1 2 3 4 5 6 7 8 9 10 $\xrightarrow{\hspace{0.3cm}}$

7. $13 > 12m + 7$

$\xleftarrow{\hspace{0.3cm}}$ $^-10$ $^-9$ $^-8$ $^-7$ $^-6$ $^-5$ $^-4$ $^-3$ $^-2$ $^-1$ 0 1 2 3 4 5 6 7 8 9 10 $\xrightarrow{\hspace{0.3cm}}$

8. $(\frac{2}{5})b \geq {^-2}$

$\xleftarrow{\hspace{0.3cm}}$ $^-10$ $^-9$ $^-8$ $^-7$ $^-6$ $^-5$ $^-4$ $^-3$ $^-2$ $^-1$ 0 1 2 3 4 5 6 7 8 9 10 $\xrightarrow{\hspace{0.3cm}}$

9. $^-\frac{r}{2} \leq 5$

$\xleftarrow{\hspace{0.3cm}}$ $^-10$ $^-9$ $^-8$ $^-7$ $^-6$ $^-5$ $^-4$ $^-3$ $^-2$ $^-1$ 0 1 2 3 4 5 6 7 8 9 10 $\xrightarrow{\hspace{0.3cm}}$

10. $^-14t > 56$

$\xleftarrow{\hspace{0.3cm}}$ $^-10$ $^-9$ $^-8$ $^-7$ $^-6$ $^-5$ $^-4$ $^-3$ $^-2$ $^-1$ 0 1 2 3 4 5 6 7 8 9 10 $\xrightarrow{\hspace{0.3cm}}$

Inequalities

Solving Inequalities

Solve each inequality and graph the answer on the number line.

1. $-14n > 98$

$-10\ -9\ -8\ -7\ -6\ -5\ -4\ -3\ -2\ -1\ 0\ 1\ 2\ 3\ 4\ 5\ 6\ 7\ 8\ 9\ 10$

2. $2.7d \geq 21.6$

$-10\ -9\ -8\ -7\ -6\ -5\ -4\ -3\ -2\ -1\ 0\ 1\ 2\ 3\ 4\ 5\ 6\ 7\ 8\ 9\ 10$

3. $w + 8.4 \geq 5.4$

$-10\ -9\ -8\ -7\ -6\ -5\ -4\ -3\ -2\ -1\ 0\ 1\ 2\ 3\ 4\ 5\ 6\ 7\ 8\ 9\ 10$

4. $\left(\frac{2}{7}\right)d \leq -2$

$-10\ -9\ -8\ -7\ -6\ -5\ -4\ -3\ -2\ -1\ 0\ 1\ 2\ 3\ 4\ 5\ 6\ 7\ 8\ 9\ 10$

5. $-3\frac{1}{8} \leq h - \frac{1}{8}$

$-10\ -9\ -8\ -7\ -6\ -5\ -4\ -3\ -2\ -1\ 0\ 1\ 2\ 3\ 4\ 5\ 6\ 7\ 8\ 9\ 10$

6. $-13.4 \geq j - 20.4$

$-10\ -9\ -8\ -7\ -6\ -5\ -4\ -3\ -2\ -1\ 0\ 1\ 2\ 3\ 4\ 5\ 6\ 7\ 8\ 9\ 10$

7. $7 > 9s + {}^-2$

$-10\ -9\ -8\ -7\ -6\ -5\ -4\ -3\ -2\ -1\ 0\ 1\ 2\ 3\ 4\ 5\ 6\ 7\ 8\ 9\ 10$

8. $-12m < m - 26$

$-10\ -9\ -8\ -7\ -6\ -5\ -4\ -3\ -2\ -1\ 0\ 1\ 2\ 3\ 4\ 5\ 6\ 7\ 8\ 9\ 10$

9. $-\frac{t}{2} \leq 2$

$-10\ -9\ -8\ -7\ -6\ -5\ -4\ -3\ -2\ -1\ 0\ 1\ 2\ 3\ 4\ 5\ 6\ 7\ 8\ 9\ 10$

10. $k + 3\frac{2}{5} \geq -1\frac{3}{5}$

$-10\ -9\ -8\ -7\ -6\ -5\ -4\ -3\ -2\ -1\ 0\ 1\ 2\ 3\ 4\ 5\ 6\ 7\ 8\ 9\ 10$

Inequalities

Solving Inequalities with Multiple Operations

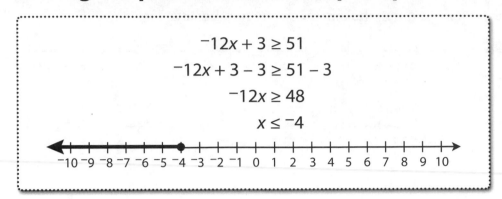

$$^-12x + 3 \geq 51$$
$$^-12x + 3 - 3 \geq 51 - 3$$
$$^-12x \geq 48$$
$$x \leq {}^-4$$

Solve each inequality and graph the answer on the number line.

1. $^-5 > 4x - 7$

2. $3(2c - 2) \geq 48$

3. $^-15 > {}^-4x - 75$

4. $^-4(4x + 4) \geq 32$

5. $5x - 9 > 21$

6. $^-2x - 10 \geq 6$

7. $20 < {}^-12.8 + 8x$

8. $^-6(3t + 3) \leq 18$

Inequalities

Solving Inequalities with Variables on Both Sides

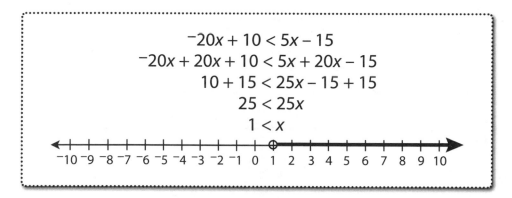

$$^-20x + 10 < 5x - 15$$
$$^-20x + 20x + 10 < 5x + 20x - 15$$
$$10 + 15 < 25x - 15 + 15$$
$$25 < 25x$$
$$1 < x$$

Solve each inequality and graph the answer on the number line.

1. $23 - 12x > ^-(7 + 2x)$

2. $3(2x - 4) > 4x + 4$

3. $3(s - 4) \geq 6s + 12$

4. $4c + 6 < (3 + 2c)$

5. $8 - e > 3e + 12$

6. $^-3(5t - 12) \leq 4t - 21$

7. $5c + 1 > 3(3 + c)$

8. $x - 4x \geq ^-5x - 10$

Inequalities

Practice Solving Inequalities

Solve each inequality and graph the answer on the number line.

1. $^-4 \geq h + 1$

2. $2.8h \leq 8.4$

3. $r + 3 \leq 5$

4. $2 \geq 2x - 8$

5. $(\frac{2}{3})k \geq {}^-6$

6. $^-13t > 78$

7. $9 \leq 6y - 15$

8. $32.7 \geq t + 25.7$

9. $^-7e \geq 21$

10. $12d < d + 11$

Inequalities

Practice Solving Inequalities

Solve each inequality and graph the answer on the number line.

1. $8c - 7 + c < 13 + 5c$

$$\text{-}10\ \text{-}9\ \text{-}8\ \text{-}7\ \text{-}6\ \text{-}5\ \text{-}4\ \text{-}3\ \text{-}2\ \text{-}1\ \ 0\ \ 1\ \ 2\ \ 3\ \ 4\ \ 5\ \ 6\ \ 7\ \ 8\ \ 9\ \ 10$$

2. $5(3w - 4) < 8w + 8$

$$\text{-}10\ \text{-}9\ \text{-}8\ \text{-}7\ \text{-}6\ \text{-}5\ \text{-}4\ \text{-}3\ \text{-}2\ \text{-}1\ \ 0\ \ 1\ \ 2\ \ 3\ \ 4\ \ 5\ \ 6\ \ 7\ \ 8\ \ 9\ \ 10$$

3. $3(4c + 3) + 1 \le 2(c - 5)$

$$\text{-}10\ \text{-}9\ \text{-}8\ \text{-}7\ \text{-}6\ \text{-}5\ \text{-}4\ \text{-}3\ \text{-}2\ \text{-}1\ \ 0\ \ 1\ \ 2\ \ 3\ \ 4\ \ 5\ \ 6\ \ 7\ \ 8\ \ 9\ \ 10$$

4. $12(m - 1) \le 5(m + 3) - 6$

$$\text{-}10\ \text{-}9\ \text{-}8\ \text{-}7\ \text{-}6\ \text{-}5\ \text{-}4\ \text{-}3\ \text{-}2\ \text{-}1\ \ 0\ \ 1\ \ 2\ \ 3\ \ 4\ \ 5\ \ 6\ \ 7\ \ 8\ \ 9\ \ 10$$

5. $\dfrac{1}{2} < (\dfrac{1}{2})x - 2$

$$\text{-}10\ \text{-}9\ \text{-}8\ \text{-}7\ \text{-}6\ \text{-}5\ \text{-}4\ \text{-}3\ \text{-}2\ \text{-}1\ \ 0\ \ 1\ \ 2\ \ 3\ \ 4\ \ 5\ \ 6\ \ 7\ \ 8\ \ 9\ \ 10$$

6. $4x + 7 < x - 8$

$$\text{-}10\ \text{-}9\ \text{-}8\ \text{-}7\ \text{-}6\ \text{-}5\ \text{-}4\ \text{-}3\ \text{-}2\ \text{-}1\ \ 0\ \ 1\ \ 2\ \ 3\ \ 4\ \ 5\ \ 6\ \ 7\ \ 8\ \ 9\ \ 10$$

7. $2(3a + 4) \ge 3a - 4$

$$\text{-}10\ \ 9\ \text{-}8\ \text{-}7\ \text{-}6\ \text{-}5\ \text{-}4\ \text{-}3\ \text{-}2\ \text{-}1\ \ 0\ \ 1\ \ 2\ \ 3\ \ 4\ \ 5\ \ 6\ \ 7\ \ 8\ \ 9\ \ 10$$

8. $48 > x + 50$

$$\text{-}10\ \text{-}9\ \text{-}8\ \text{-}7\ \text{-}6\ \text{-}5\ \text{-}4\ \text{-}3\ \text{-}2\ \text{-}1\ \ 0\ \ 1\ \ 2\ \ 3\ \ 4\ \ 5\ \ 6\ \ 7\ \ 8\ \ 9\ \ 10$$

9. $\text{-}5(4a + 4) \ge 40$

$$\text{-}10\ \text{-}9\ \text{-}8\ \text{-}7\ \text{-}6\ \text{-}5\ \text{-}4\ \text{-}3\ \text{-}2\ \text{-}1\ \ 0\ \ 1\ \ 2\ \ 3\ \ 4\ \ 5\ \ 6\ \ 7\ \ 8\ \ 9\ \ 10$$

10. $11x \ge \text{-}44$

$$\text{-}10\ \text{-}9\ \text{-}8\ \text{-}7\ \text{-}6\ \text{-}5\ \text{-}4\ \text{-}3\ \text{-}2\ \text{-}1\ \ 0\ \ 1\ \ 2\ \ 3\ \ 4\ \ 5\ \ 6\ \ 7\ \ 8\ \ 9\ \ 10$$

Ordered Pairs and Graphing

Plotting Points

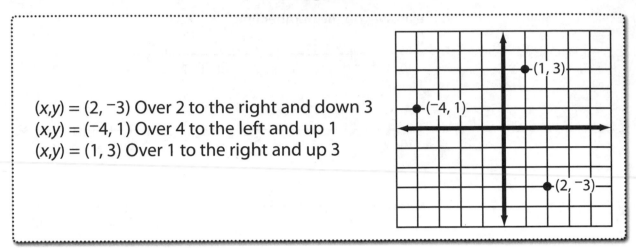

$(x,y) = (2, {}^{-}3)$ Over 2 to the right and down 3
$(x,y) = ({}^{-}4, 1)$ Over 4 to the left and up 1
$(x,y) = (1, 3)$ Over 1 to the right and up 3

Plot and label the following points on the graph.

A $(3, {}^{-}4)$

B $(6, 2)$

C $(0, {}^{-}2)$

D $(1, 7)$

E $(3, {}^{-}3)$

F $(2, {}^{-}6)$

G $({}^{-}3, 4)$

H $({}^{-}1, {}^{-}4)$

I $(3, 0)$

J $(2, 5)$

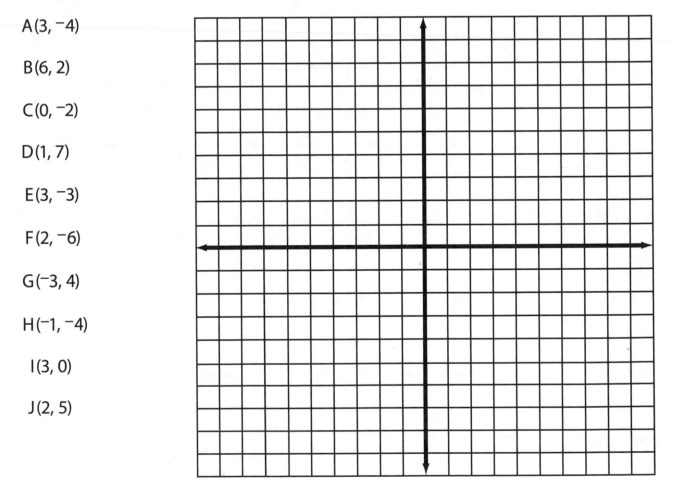

Ordered Pairs and Graphing

Plotting Points

$y - 6 = 8x$ Let $x = {}^-1, {}^-2, 2$
$y - 6 + 6 = 8x + 6$ Solve for y.
$y = 8x + 6$

$x = {}^-1$	$x = {}^-2$	$x = 2$
$y = 8({}^-1) + 6$	$x = 8({}^-2) + 6$	$x = 8(2) + 6$
$y = {}^-8 + 6$	$x = {}^-16 + 6$	$x = 16 + 6$
$y = {}^-2$	$x = {}^-10$	$x = 22$
$({}^-1, {}^-2)$	$({}^-2, {}^-10)$	$(2, 22)$

Use the given value for x to solve each equation for y. Write the answer as an ordered pairs.

1. $2 = y - 4x$, Let $x = {}^-1, 0, 2$

2. $^-x = y - 4$, Let $x = {}^-1, {}^-2, {}^-3$

3. $2x + y = {}^-5$, Let $x = {}^-3, 2, 4$

4. $2 = y - 3x$, Let $x = {}^-1, 0, 2$

5. $4 - y = 2x$, Let $x = {}^-3, 1, {}^-2$

6. $2x + y = 5$, Let $x = {}^-4, 0, 2$

7. $4x - y = {}^-10$, Let $x = 2, 3, {}^-2$

8. $4x - 2y = b$, Let $x = {}^-1, \frac{1}{2}, 2$

Ordered Pairs and Graphing

Graphing Linear Equations

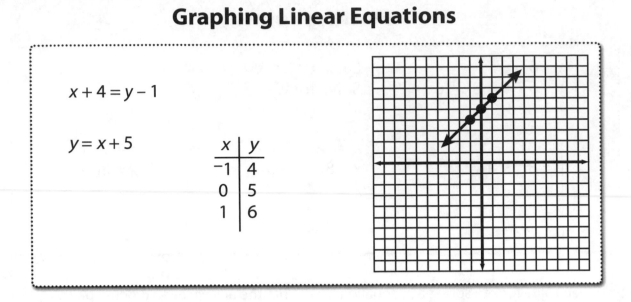

$x + 4 = y - 1$

$y = x + 5$

x	y
−1	4
0	5
1	6

Choose 3 values for x and find the values for y. Graph each ordered pair and draw a line connecting them.

1. $y + 3 = 3x$

x	y

2. $2y = 4x + 4$

x	y

Ordered Pairs and Graphing

Graphing Linear Equations

Choose 3 values for *x* and find the values for *y*. Graph each ordered pair and draw a line connecting them.

1. $y - 4 = 2x$

2. $y + 4 = 3x$

3. $4x - y = 8$

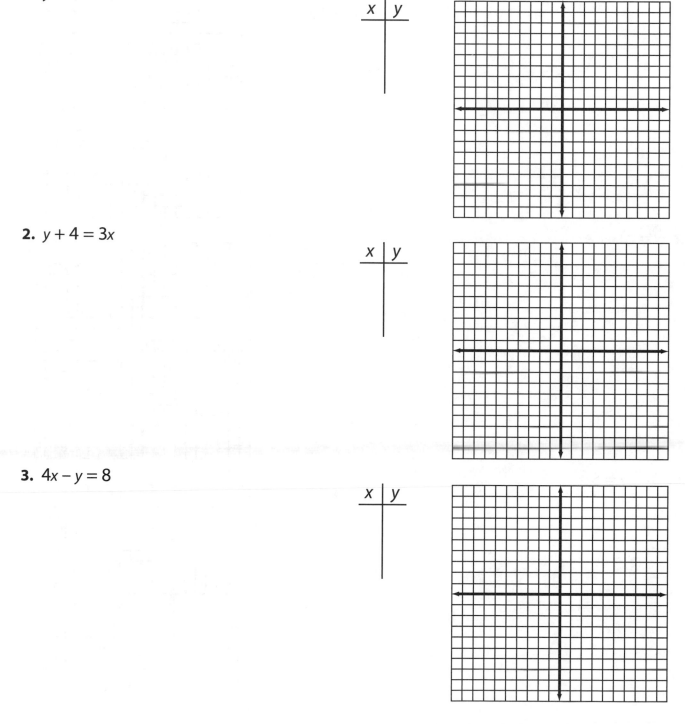

Ordered Pairs and Graphing

Graphing Linear Equations

Choose 3 values for *x* and find the values for *y*. Graph each ordered pair and draw a line connecting them.

1. $4x - y = 5$

2. $y = {}^-3x + 4$

3. $3x - y = 5$

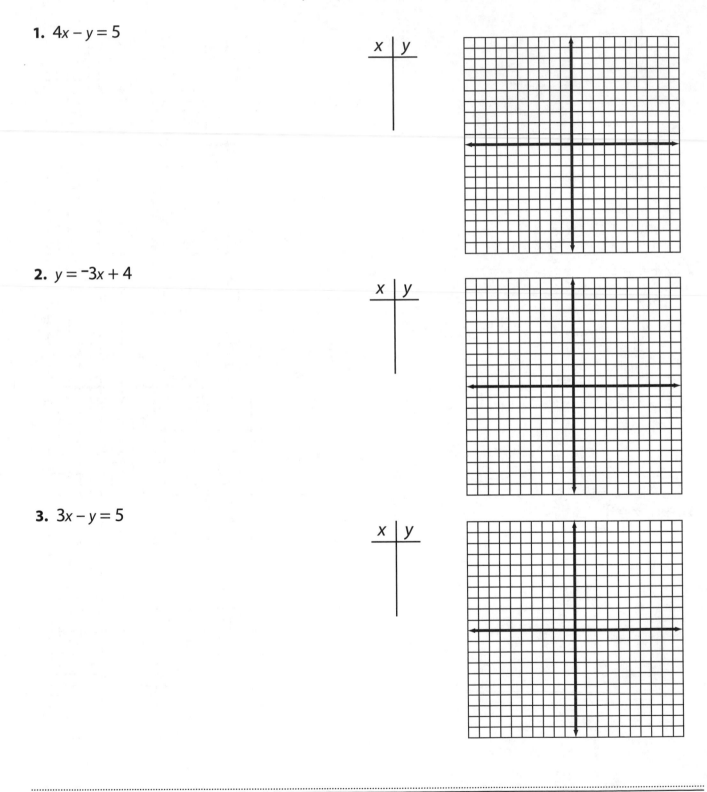

Name _____   Date _____

Ordered Pairs and Graphing

Graphing Linear Equations

Choose 3 values for *x* and find the values for *y*. Graph each ordered pair and draw a line connecting them.

1. $2x + y = 3$

2. $y = {}^-3x$

3. $^-x + y = {}^-5$

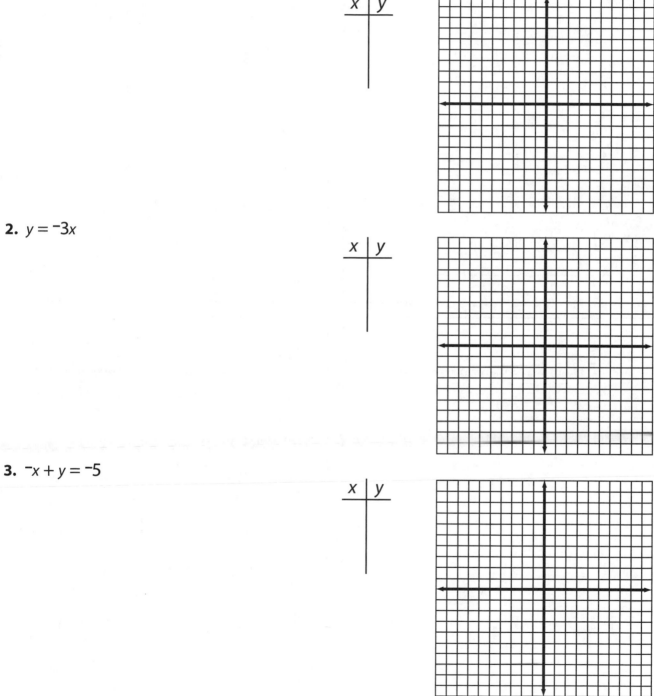

Name _____ Date _____

Fractions

Simplifying Fractions

$$\frac{3}{6} \div \frac{3}{3} \text{ (greatest common factor)} = \frac{1}{2}$$

Simplify each fraction by dividing by the greatest common factor.

1. $\frac{5}{15}$ **$\frac{1}{3}$** 2. $\frac{8}{24}$ **$\frac{1}{3}$** 3. $\frac{10}{70}$ **$\frac{1}{7}$**

4. $\frac{13}{39}$ **$\frac{1}{3}$** 5. $\frac{19}{57}$ **$\frac{1}{3}$** 6. $\frac{54}{63}$ **$\frac{6}{7}$**

7. $\frac{6}{39}$ **$\frac{2}{13}$** 8. $\frac{6}{15}$ **$\frac{2}{5}$** 9. $\frac{7}{42}$ **$\frac{1}{6}$**

10. $\frac{35}{35}$ **1** 11. $\frac{9}{36}$ **$\frac{1}{4}$** 12. $\frac{45}{72}$ **$\frac{5}{8}$**

13. $\frac{32}{136}$ **$\frac{4}{17}$** 14. $\frac{6}{48}$ **$\frac{1}{8}$** 15. $\frac{30}{45}$ **$\frac{2}{3}$**

16. $\frac{27}{81}$ **$\frac{1}{3}$** 17. $\frac{56}{74}$ **$\frac{28}{37}$** 18. $\frac{16}{72}$ **$\frac{2}{9}$**

19. $\frac{56}{63}$ **$\frac{8}{9}$** 20. $\frac{7}{70}$ **$\frac{1}{10}$** 21. $\frac{12}{18}$ **$\frac{2}{3}$**

CD-104315 • © Carson-Dellosa

Name _____ Date _____

Fractions

Simplifying Fractions

$$\frac{18}{14} \div \frac{2}{2} = \frac{9}{7}$$
Improper Fraction

$$\frac{18}{14} \div \frac{2}{2} = \frac{9}{7} = \frac{7}{7} + \frac{2}{7} = 1 + \frac{2}{7} = 1\frac{2}{7}$$
Mixed Number

Simplify each improper fraction. Then, write each reduced improper fraction as a mixed number.

1. $\frac{15}{9}$ **$\frac{5}{3}$** = **$1\frac{2}{3}$** 2. $\frac{36}{24}$ **$\frac{3}{2}$** = **$1\frac{1}{2}$**

3. $\frac{28}{20}$ **$\frac{7}{5}$** = **$1\frac{2}{5}$** 4. $\frac{66}{19}$ **$\frac{66}{19}$** = **$3\frac{9}{19}$**

5. $\frac{45}{27}$ **$\frac{5}{3}$** = **$1\frac{2}{3}$** 6. $\frac{27}{21}$ **$\frac{9}{7}$** = **$1\frac{2}{7}$**

7. $\frac{45}{36}$ **$\frac{5}{4}$** = **$1\frac{1}{4}$** 8. $\frac{69}{18}$ **$\frac{23}{6}$** = **$3\frac{5}{6}$**

9. $\frac{22}{8}$ **$\frac{11}{4}$** = **$2\frac{3}{4}$** 10. $\frac{36}{10}$ **$\frac{18}{5}$** = **$3\frac{3}{5}$**

11. $\frac{20}{12}$ **$\frac{5}{3}$** = **$1\frac{2}{3}$** 12. $\frac{27}{24}$ **$\frac{9}{8}$** = **$1\frac{1}{8}$**

13. $\frac{50}{30}$ **$\frac{5}{3}$** = **$1\frac{2}{3}$** 14. $\frac{30}{12}$ **$\frac{5}{2}$** = **$2\frac{1}{2}$**

CD-104315 • © Carson-Dellosa

Name _____ Date _____

Fractions

Adding and Subtracting Fractions with Like Denominators

$$\frac{1}{8} + \frac{3}{8} = \frac{4}{8} = \frac{1}{2} \qquad \frac{5}{8} - \frac{1}{8} = \frac{4}{8} = \frac{1}{2}$$

Add or subtract. Write the answer in simplest form.

1. $\frac{4}{15} - \frac{1}{15} =$ **$\frac{1}{5}$** 2. $\frac{11}{12} + \frac{9}{12} =$ **$1\frac{2}{3}$** 3. $\frac{19}{20} - \frac{17}{20} =$ **$\frac{1}{10}$**

4. $\frac{17}{18} - \frac{8}{18} =$ **$\frac{1}{2}$** 5. $\frac{13}{30} + \frac{11}{30} =$ **$\frac{4}{5}$** 6. $\frac{32}{35} - \frac{17}{35} =$ **$\frac{3}{7}$**

7. $\frac{13}{24} + \frac{17}{24} =$ **$1\frac{1}{4}$** 8. $\frac{3}{21} + \frac{11}{21} =$ **$\frac{2}{3}$** 9. $\frac{16}{18} + \frac{17}{18} =$ **$1\frac{5}{6}$**

10. $\frac{11}{14} - \frac{6}{14} =$ **$\frac{5}{14}$** 11. $\frac{31}{32} + \frac{29}{32} =$ **$1\frac{7}{8}$** 12. $\frac{19}{20} - \frac{9}{20} =$ **$\frac{1}{2}$**

13. $\frac{2}{9} + \frac{3}{9} =$ **$\frac{5}{9}$** 14. $\frac{6}{8} + \frac{7}{8} =$ **$1\frac{5}{8}$** 15. $\frac{19}{24} + \frac{23}{24} =$ **$1\frac{3}{4}$**

16. $\frac{23}{25} - \frac{8}{25} =$ **$\frac{3}{5}$** 17. $\frac{13}{15} - \frac{11}{15} =$ **$\frac{2}{15}$** 18. $\frac{16}{17} - \frac{9}{17} =$ **$\frac{7}{17}$**

CD-104315 • © Carson-Dellosa

Name _____ Date _____

Fractions

Adding and Subtracting Fractions with Unlike Denominators

$$\frac{3}{7} + \frac{2}{6} = \frac{18}{42} + \frac{14}{42} = \frac{32}{42} = \frac{16}{21} \qquad \frac{3}{7} - \frac{2}{6} = \frac{18}{42} - \frac{14}{42} = \frac{4}{42} = \frac{2}{21}$$

Solve each problem. Write the answer in simplest form.

1. $\frac{6}{7} + \frac{1}{5} =$ **$1\frac{2}{35}$** 2. $\frac{4}{9} - \frac{1}{3} =$ **$\frac{1}{9}$** 3. $\frac{3}{4} + \frac{2}{9} =$ **$\frac{35}{36}$**

4. $\frac{5}{6} + \frac{7}{8} =$ **$1\frac{17}{24}$** 5. $\frac{1}{6} + \frac{7}{9} =$ **$\frac{17}{18}$** 6. $\frac{9}{25} - \frac{3}{10} =$ **$\frac{3}{50}$**

7. $\frac{2}{3} - \frac{5}{8} =$ **$\frac{1}{24}$** 8. $\frac{5}{8} + \frac{11}{12} =$ **$1\frac{13}{24}$** 9. $\frac{2}{5} - \frac{3}{8} =$ **$\frac{1}{40}$**

10. $\frac{1}{6} + \frac{3}{4} =$ **$\frac{11}{12}$** 11. $\frac{9}{10} - \frac{7}{20} =$ **$\frac{11}{20}$** 12. $\frac{5}{10} + \frac{6}{8} =$ **$1\frac{1}{4}$**

13. $\frac{8}{9} - \frac{5}{12} =$ **$\frac{17}{36}$** 14. $\frac{2}{3} - \frac{2}{5} =$ **$\frac{4}{15}$** 15. $\frac{1}{4} + \frac{4}{8} =$ **$\frac{3}{4}$**

16. $\frac{4}{9} + \frac{7}{8} =$ **$1\frac{23}{72}$** 17. $\frac{2}{4} + \frac{3}{7} =$ **$\frac{13}{14}$** 18. $\frac{7}{10} - \frac{3}{8} =$ **$\frac{13}{40}$**

CD-104315 • © Carson-Dellosa

Name _____ Date _____

Fractions

Adding and Subtracting Fractions with Unlike Denominators

$$\frac{4}{6} + \frac{3}{5} = \frac{20}{30} + \frac{18}{30} = \frac{38}{30} = 1\frac{4}{15} \qquad \frac{4}{6} - \frac{3}{5} = \frac{20}{30} - \frac{18}{30} = \frac{2}{30} = \frac{1}{15}$$

Solve each problem. Write the answer in simplest form.

1. $\frac{2}{6} + \frac{3}{9} = \mathbf{\frac{2}{3}}$ 2. $\frac{11}{12} - \frac{5}{18} = \mathbf{\frac{23}{36}}$ 3. $\frac{8}{12} + \frac{7}{8} = \mathbf{1\frac{13}{24}}$

4. $\frac{17}{21} - \frac{4}{6} = \mathbf{\frac{1}{7}}$ 5. $\frac{3}{10} + \frac{7}{15} = \mathbf{\frac{23}{30}}$ 6. $\frac{11}{12} - \frac{3}{6} = \mathbf{\frac{5}{12}}$

7. $\frac{7}{15} + \frac{3}{6} = \mathbf{\frac{29}{30}}$ 8. $\frac{5}{6} - \frac{3}{9} = \mathbf{\frac{1}{2}}$ 9. $\frac{6}{7} - \frac{3}{5} = \mathbf{\frac{9}{35}}$

10. $\frac{11}{15} + \frac{1}{6} = \mathbf{\frac{9}{10}}$ 11. $\frac{5}{8} + \frac{2}{7} = \mathbf{\frac{51}{56}}$ 12. $\frac{29}{32} + \frac{7}{8} = \mathbf{1\frac{25}{32}}$

13. $\frac{4}{9} + \frac{11}{15} = \mathbf{1\frac{8}{15}}$ 14. $\frac{5}{15} - \frac{3}{10} = \mathbf{\frac{1}{30}}$ 15. $\frac{11}{14} - \frac{1}{6} = \mathbf{\frac{13}{21}}$

16. $\frac{8}{9} + \frac{4}{5} = \mathbf{1\frac{31}{45}}$ 17. $\frac{7}{8} + \frac{8}{9} = \mathbf{1\frac{55}{72}}$ 18. $\frac{11}{12} - \frac{5}{15} = \mathbf{\frac{7}{12}}$

8   CD-104315 • © Carson-Dellosa

Name _____ Date _____

Fractions

Adding and Subtracting Mixed Numbers

$$3\frac{1}{2} + 1\frac{3}{8} = 3\frac{4}{8} + 1\frac{3}{8} = 4\frac{7}{8}$$

Solve each problem. Write the answer in simplest form.

1. $4\frac{5}{7} - 2\frac{2}{3} = \mathbf{2\frac{1}{21}}$ 2. $9\frac{3}{5} + 4\frac{2}{3} = \mathbf{14\frac{4}{15}}$ 3. $7\frac{1}{2} - 2\frac{7}{10} = \mathbf{4\frac{4}{5}}$

4. $17\frac{3}{4} - 8\frac{2}{5} = \mathbf{9\frac{7}{20}}$ 5. $16\frac{1}{4} - 7\frac{5}{8} = \mathbf{8\frac{5}{8}}$ 6. $6\frac{2}{7} - 1\frac{1}{3} = \mathbf{4\frac{20}{21}}$

7. $3\frac{7}{12} + 7\frac{5}{6} = \mathbf{11\frac{5}{12}}$ 8. $4\frac{1}{8} - 3\frac{1}{2} = \mathbf{\frac{5}{8}}$ 9. $8\frac{1}{8} + 5\frac{3}{4} = \mathbf{13\frac{7}{8}}$

10. $12\frac{7}{9} + 3\frac{2}{3} = \mathbf{16\frac{4}{9}}$ 11. $4\frac{1}{7} - 3\frac{1}{5} = \mathbf{\frac{33}{35}}$ 12. $6\frac{4}{5} + 2\frac{3}{9} = \mathbf{9\frac{2}{15}}$

13. $1\frac{9}{12} - 1\frac{3}{4} = \mathbf{0}$ 14. $4\frac{8}{9} + 2\frac{5}{6} = \mathbf{7\frac{13}{18}}$ 15. $4\frac{3}{6} + 7\frac{3}{8} = \mathbf{11\frac{7}{8}}$

16. $5\frac{1}{2} - 2\frac{2}{7} = \mathbf{3\frac{3}{14}}$ 17. $2\frac{8}{10} - 1\frac{5}{15} = \mathbf{1\frac{7}{15}}$ 18. $11\frac{4}{5} - 3\frac{5}{6} = \mathbf{7\frac{29}{30}}$

CD-104315 • © Carson-Dellosa   9

Name _____ Date _____

Fractions

Adding and Subtracting Mixed Numbers Practice

$$2\frac{2}{3} + 6\frac{4}{5} = 2\frac{10}{15} + 6\frac{12}{15} = 8\frac{22}{15} = 9\frac{7}{15}$$

Solve each problem. Write the answer in simplest form.

1. $6\frac{2}{3} - 5\frac{3}{9} = \mathbf{1\frac{1}{3}}$ 2. $6\frac{8}{12} - 5\frac{1}{3} = \mathbf{1\frac{1}{3}}$ 3. $5\frac{5}{9} + 3\frac{4}{6} = \mathbf{9\frac{2}{9}}$

4. $9\frac{5}{9} - 6\frac{1}{2} = \mathbf{3\frac{1}{18}}$ 5. $14\frac{3}{4} - 8\frac{5}{6} = \mathbf{5\frac{11}{12}}$ 6. $5\frac{2}{9} + 3\frac{3}{6} = \mathbf{8\frac{13}{18}}$

7. $7\frac{3}{12} + 4\frac{1}{8} = \mathbf{11\frac{3}{8}}$ 8. $6\frac{7}{8} - 4\frac{2}{9} = \mathbf{2\frac{47}{72}}$ 9. $8\frac{1}{3} + 6\frac{7}{6} = \mathbf{15\frac{1}{2}}$

10. $5\frac{2}{7} - 3\frac{5}{6} = \mathbf{1\frac{19}{42}}$ 11. $13\frac{4}{21} - 8\frac{2}{3} = \mathbf{4\frac{11}{21}}$ 12. $9\frac{8}{11} + 4\frac{1}{2} = \mathbf{14\frac{5}{22}}$

13. $5\frac{1}{3} - 3\frac{5}{6} = \mathbf{1\frac{1}{2}}$ 14. $4\frac{3}{10} - 2\frac{9}{12} = \mathbf{1\frac{11}{20}}$ 15. $4\frac{10}{12} - 3\frac{4}{6} = \mathbf{1\frac{1}{6}}$

16. $7\frac{7}{12} - 3\frac{2}{3} = \mathbf{3\frac{11}{12}}$ 17. $3\frac{15}{18} + 2\frac{4}{12} = \mathbf{6\frac{1}{6}}$ 18. $3\frac{2}{3} + 6\frac{3}{5} = \mathbf{10\frac{4}{15}}$

10   CD-104315 • © Carson-Dellosa

Name _____ Date _____

Fractions

Multiplying Fractions

$$1\frac{1}{5} \times 2\frac{1}{2} = \frac{7}{5} \times \frac{5}{2} = \frac{35}{10} \text{ or } 3\frac{5}{10} = 3\frac{1}{2}$$

Solve each problem. Write the answer in simplest form.

1. $10\frac{3}{3} \times 7\frac{1}{8} = \mathbf{76}$ 2. $5\frac{4}{7} \times 1\frac{2}{3} = \mathbf{9\frac{2}{7}}$ 3. $4\frac{5}{6} \times 5\frac{1}{7} = \mathbf{24\frac{6}{7}}$

4. $\frac{3}{5} \times \frac{15}{18} = \mathbf{\frac{1}{2}}$ 5. $8\frac{1}{3} \times 6\frac{3}{5} = \mathbf{55}$ 6. $2\frac{11}{13} \times 4\frac{2}{3} = \mathbf{13\frac{11}{39}}$

7. $5\frac{1}{2} \times \frac{3}{11} = \mathbf{1\frac{1}{2}}$ 8. $3\frac{1}{5} \times 12\frac{1}{2} = \mathbf{40}$ 9. $5\frac{2}{3} \times 8\frac{1}{4} = \mathbf{46\frac{3}{4}}$

10. $7\frac{2}{7} \times 2\frac{1}{3} = \mathbf{17}$ 11. $1\frac{1}{3} \times 3\frac{3}{5} = \mathbf{4\frac{4}{5}}$ 12. $\frac{2}{3} \times \frac{21}{24} = \mathbf{\frac{7}{12}}$

13. $5\frac{3}{5} \times 2\frac{4}{7} = \mathbf{14\frac{2}{5}}$ 14. $7\frac{2}{3} \times 3\frac{1}{2} = \mathbf{26\frac{5}{6}}$ 15. $5\frac{3}{12} \times 2\frac{1}{7} = \mathbf{11\frac{1}{4}}$

16. $9\frac{1}{3} \times 2\frac{1}{7} = \mathbf{20}$ 17. $2\frac{3}{5} \times 1\frac{1}{4} = \mathbf{3\frac{1}{4}}$ 18. $2\frac{4}{7} \times 2\frac{3}{9} = \mathbf{6}$

CD-104315 • © Carson-Dellosa   11

Sheet 1 — Multiplying Fractions

Name _____ Date _____

Fractions

Multiplying Fractions

$$2\frac{2}{3} \times 1\frac{1}{4} = \frac{8}{3} \times \frac{5}{4} = \frac{40}{12} = \frac{10}{3} \text{ or } 3\frac{1}{3}$$

Solve each problem. Write the answer in simplest form.

1. $4\frac{1}{4} \times 5\frac{3}{5} = \mathbf{23\frac{4}{5}}$
2. $3\frac{1}{3} \times 9\frac{3}{4} = \mathbf{32\frac{1}{2}}$
3. $8\frac{2}{5} \times 3\frac{4}{7} = \mathbf{30}$

4. $8\frac{1}{3} \times 2\frac{4}{7} = \mathbf{21\frac{3}{7}}$
5. $7\frac{1}{3} \times 4\frac{1}{2} = \mathbf{33}$
6. $15\frac{3}{4} \times 6\frac{2}{7} = \mathbf{99}$

7. $13\frac{1}{3} \times 2\frac{2}{5} = \mathbf{32}$
8. $5\frac{3}{4} \times 4\frac{4}{5} = \mathbf{27\frac{3}{5}}$
9. $8\frac{4}{5} \times 2\frac{5}{10} = \mathbf{22}$

10. $6\frac{2}{9} \times 2\frac{2}{3} = \mathbf{16\frac{16}{27}}$
11. $3\frac{3}{5} \times 2\frac{7}{9} = \mathbf{10}$
12. $4\frac{7}{12} \times 6\frac{2}{5} = \mathbf{29\frac{1}{3}}$

13. $7\frac{1}{8} \times 9\frac{1}{3} = \mathbf{66\frac{1}{2}}$
14. $4\frac{2}{3} \times 7\frac{1}{2} = \mathbf{35}$
15. $5\frac{4}{9} \times 2\frac{4}{7} = \mathbf{14}$

16. $10\frac{1}{2} \times 7\frac{1}{3} = \mathbf{77}$
17. $3\frac{8}{9} \times 2\frac{1}{5} = \mathbf{8\frac{5}{9}}$
18. $12\frac{1}{2} \times 8\frac{2}{5} = \mathbf{105}$

12   CD-104315 • © Carson-Dellosa

Sheet 2 — Dividing Fractions

Name _____ Date _____

Fractions

Dividing Fractions

$$1\frac{2}{3} \div 2\frac{1}{5} = \frac{5}{3} \div \frac{11}{5} = \frac{5}{3} \times \frac{5}{11} = \frac{25}{33}$$

Solve each problem. Write the answer in simplest form.

1. $6\frac{2}{3} \div 4\frac{4}{9} = \mathbf{1\frac{1}{2}}$
2. $3\frac{1}{3} \div 1\frac{5}{9} = \mathbf{2\frac{1}{7}}$
3. $2\frac{7}{10} \div 3\frac{9}{15} = \mathbf{\frac{3}{4}}$

4. $4\frac{1}{2} \div 5\frac{1}{4} = \mathbf{\frac{6}{7}}$
5. $6\frac{3}{4} \div 2\frac{1}{2} = \mathbf{2\frac{7}{10}}$
6. $2\frac{2}{6} \div 4\frac{2}{3} = \mathbf{\frac{1}{2}}$

7. $5\frac{2}{5} \div 4\frac{1}{2} = \mathbf{1\frac{1}{5}}$
8. $7\frac{2}{7} \div 2\frac{2}{14} = \mathbf{3\frac{2}{5}}$
9. $3\frac{1}{2} \div 4\frac{1}{3} = \mathbf{\frac{21}{26}}$

10. $2\frac{2}{3} \div 3\frac{4}{10} = \mathbf{\frac{40}{51}}$
11. $4\frac{1}{5} \div 3\frac{3}{5} = \mathbf{1\frac{1}{6}}$
12. $5\frac{3}{5} \div 1\frac{5}{9} = \mathbf{3\frac{3}{5}}$

13. $4\frac{3}{8} \div 2\frac{1}{12} = \mathbf{2\frac{1}{10}}$
14. $7\frac{3}{4} \div 1\frac{1}{4} = \mathbf{6\frac{1}{5}}$
15. $3\frac{3}{4} \div 1\frac{2}{3} = \mathbf{2\frac{1}{4}}$

16. $3\frac{1}{5} \div 1\frac{6}{10} = \mathbf{2}$
17. $2\frac{2}{9} \div 4\frac{1}{6} = \mathbf{\frac{8}{15}}$
18. $4\frac{3}{5} \div 1\frac{3}{8} = \mathbf{3\frac{19}{55}}$

CD-104315 • © Carson-Dellosa   13

Sheet 3 — Dividing Fractions

Name _____ Date _____

Fractions

Dividing Fractions

$$1\frac{1}{8} \div 2\frac{1}{6} = \frac{9}{8} \div \frac{13}{6} = \frac{9}{8} \times \frac{6}{13} = \frac{27}{52}$$

Solve each problem. Write the answer in simplest form.

1. $9\frac{1}{6} \div 3\frac{5}{12} = \mathbf{2\frac{28}{41}}$
2. $9\frac{1}{6} \div 3\frac{8}{12} = \mathbf{2\frac{1}{2}}$
3. $7\frac{1}{2} \div 8\frac{3}{4} = \mathbf{\frac{6}{7}}$

4. $5\frac{1}{2} \div 8\frac{4}{5} = \mathbf{\frac{5}{8}}$
5. $5\frac{4}{5} \div 1\frac{8}{15} = \mathbf{3\frac{18}{23}}$
6. $9\frac{1}{5} \div 2\frac{3}{10} = \mathbf{4}$

7. $7\frac{4}{5} \div 1\frac{3}{10} = \mathbf{6}$
8. $7\frac{1}{9} \div 2\frac{2}{3} = \mathbf{2\frac{2}{3}}$
9. $8\frac{4}{5} \div 1\frac{1}{15} = \mathbf{8\frac{1}{4}}$

10. $8\frac{2}{5} \div 2\frac{1}{10} = \mathbf{4}$
11. $5\frac{3}{5} \div 1\frac{6}{10} = \mathbf{3\frac{1}{2}}$
12. $6\frac{1}{3} \div 2\frac{1}{6} = \mathbf{2\frac{12}{13}}$

13. $11\frac{3}{4} \div 5\frac{1}{2} = \mathbf{2\frac{3}{22}}$
14. $8\frac{3}{5} \div 2\frac{7}{10} = \mathbf{3\frac{5}{27}}$
15. $3\frac{5}{7} \div 3\frac{13}{14} = \mathbf{\frac{52}{55}}$

16. $3\frac{3}{4} \div 3\frac{1}{8} = \mathbf{1\frac{1}{5}}$
17. $9\frac{3}{7} \div 5\frac{10}{14} = \mathbf{1\frac{13}{20}}$
18. $5\frac{1}{6} \div 2\frac{1}{12} = \mathbf{2\frac{12}{25}}$

14   CD-104315 • © Carson-Dellosa

Sheet 4 — Mixed Practice with Fractions

Name _____ Date _____

Fractions

Mixed Practice with Fractions

Solve each problem. Write the answer in simplest form.

1. $5\frac{1}{3} \div 2\frac{4}{12} = \mathbf{2\frac{2}{7}}$
2. $7\frac{1}{2} + 6\frac{3}{4} = \mathbf{14\frac{1}{4}}$
3. $4\frac{4}{5} \times 3\frac{3}{4} = \mathbf{18}$

4. $15\frac{3}{4} \times 3\frac{3}{7} = \mathbf{54}$
5. $\frac{3}{5} \div \frac{4}{5} = \mathbf{\frac{3}{4}}$
6. $5\frac{3}{5} + 8\frac{1}{4} = \mathbf{13\frac{17}{20}}$

7. $11\frac{1}{7} - 7\frac{5}{6} = \mathbf{3\frac{13}{42}}$
8. $7\frac{1}{2} - 2\frac{3}{7} = \mathbf{5\frac{1}{14}}$
9. $7\frac{3}{5} + 4\frac{7}{8} = \mathbf{12\frac{19}{40}}$

10. $7\frac{1}{2} \div 4\frac{1}{6} = \mathbf{1\frac{4}{5}}$
11. $4\frac{6}{3} + 6\frac{2}{3} = \mathbf{12\frac{2}{3}}$
12. $4\frac{2}{15} - 1\frac{11}{12} = \mathbf{2\frac{13}{60}}$

13. $\frac{7}{8} \times \frac{3}{14} = \mathbf{\frac{3}{16}}$
14. $9\frac{3}{5} \div 3\frac{6}{10} = \mathbf{2\frac{2}{3}}$
15. $15\frac{5}{6} + 3\frac{4}{9} = \mathbf{19\frac{5}{18}}$

16. $8 - 3\frac{2}{7} = \mathbf{4\frac{5}{7}}$
17. $6\frac{6}{15} - 2\frac{4}{15} = \mathbf{4\frac{2}{15}}$
18. $5\frac{5}{8} \times 5\frac{1}{3} = \mathbf{30}$

19. $8\frac{6}{30} + 6\frac{5}{15} = \mathbf{14\frac{8}{15}}$
20. $3\frac{1}{2} \times 8\frac{4}{5} = \mathbf{30\frac{4}{5}}$
21. $4\frac{2}{5} \div 3\frac{3}{10} = \mathbf{1\frac{1}{3}}$

CD-104315 • © Carson-Dellosa   15

Name _____ Date _____

Fractions

Problem Solving with Fractions

Solve each problem. Show your work. Write the answer in simplest form.

1. Katie wants to make muffins for a school party. The recipe calls for $5\frac{1}{2}$ cups of flour. A 16-ounce bag of flour contains 2 cups. How many bags of flour must Katie purchase to make the cookies?

   3 bags

2. A banana bread recipe calls for $1\frac{2}{3}$ cups of flour, $1\frac{1}{3}$ cups of sugar, $\frac{2}{3}$ cups of sliced bananas, and $2\frac{2}{3}$ cups of walnuts. How many cups of ingredients are needed to make the banana bread?

   $6\frac{1}{3}$ cups

3. If $2\frac{1}{2}$ pounds of pecans cost $2.10 and $2\frac{1}{3}$ pounds of almonds cost $2.60, which nut is less expensive per pound?

   pecans

4. Marta brought her lunch to school 15 days out of the month of May. Out of these days, she brought carrot sticks $\frac{2}{5}$ of the time. How many days did she bring carrot sticks in May?

   6 days

5. Josie is making fruit salad for a party. She bought $1\frac{1}{2}$ pounds of apples, $1\frac{3}{4}$ pounds of cherries, and $2\frac{2}{3}$ pounds of grapes. How many pounds of fruit did Josie buy in all?

   $5\frac{11}{12}$

6. A cake recipe calls for $\frac{1}{2}$ cups of flour, $\frac{2}{3}$ cup of water, $\frac{1}{5}$ cup of salt. How many cups of ingredients are needed to make the cake?

   $1\frac{11}{30}$ cups

16   CD-104315 • © Carson-Dellosa

Name _____ Date _____

Decimals

Writing Fractions as Decimals

$$\frac{1}{5} \longrightarrow 5\overline{)1.00} \longrightarrow \frac{1}{5} = 0.2 \qquad \frac{1}{3} \longrightarrow 3\overline{)1.00} \longrightarrow \frac{1}{3} = 0.\overline{3}$$
Terminating   Repeating

Write each fraction as a decimal. Draw a line above repeating numbers in decimals.

1. $\frac{2}{3}$ **$0.\overline{6}$**   2. $\frac{1}{2}$ **0.5**   3. $\frac{4}{33}$ **$0.\overline{12}$**

4. $\frac{13}{15}$ **$0.8\overline{6}$**   5. $\frac{28}{35}$ **0.8**   6. $\frac{6}{15}$ **0.4**

7. $\frac{11}{22}$ **0.5**   8. $\frac{1}{9}$ **$0.\overline{1}$**   9. $\frac{2}{10}$ **0.2**

10. $\frac{8}{16}$ **0.5**   11. $\frac{23}{33}$ **$0.\overline{69}$**   12. $\frac{12}{25}$ **0.48**

13. $3\frac{2}{3}$ **$3.\overline{6}$**   14. $\frac{7}{16}$ **0.4375**   15. $2\frac{3}{5}$ **2.6**

CD-104315 • © Carson-Dellosa   17

Name _____ Date _____

Decimals

Writing Fractions as Decimals

Write each fraction as a decimal. Draw a line above repeating numbers in decimals.

1. $\frac{9}{36}$ **0.25**   2. $\frac{8}{15}$ **$0.5\overline{3}$**   3. $\frac{30}{45}$ **$0.\overline{6}$**

4. $\frac{19}{57}$ **$0.\overline{3}$**   5. $\frac{45}{72}$ **0.625**   6. $\frac{21}{36}$ **$0.58\overline{3}$**

7. $\frac{10}{60}$ **$0.1\overline{6}$**   8. $\frac{32}{36}$ **$0.\overline{8}$**   9. $\frac{56}{63}$ **$0.\overline{8}$**

10. $\frac{13}{39}$ **$0.\overline{3}$**   11. $\frac{5}{10}$ **0.5**   12. $\frac{12}{18}$ **$0.\overline{6}$**

13. $\frac{8}{24}$ **$0.\overline{3}$**   14. $\frac{56}{64}$ **0.875**   15. $\frac{48}{74}$ **$0.\overline{648}$**

16. $\frac{6}{22}$ **$0.\overline{27}$**   17. $\frac{16}{72}$ **$0.\overline{2}$**   18. $\frac{35}{55}$ **$0.\overline{63}$**

19. $\frac{6}{40}$ **0.15**   20. $\frac{4}{36}$ **$0.\overline{1}$**   21. $\frac{7}{48}$ **$0.145\overline{83}$**

18   CD-104315 • © Carson-Dellosa

Name _____ Date _____

Decimals

Rounding Decimals

Round 15.443 to the nearest tenth.
15.4④3 ⟶ 4 < 5 therefore 15.443 = 15.4

Round 22.72 to the nearest whole number.
22.⑦2 ⟶ 7 > 5 therefore 22.72 = 23

Round each decimal to the nearest whole number.

1. 13.398 **13**   2. 29.88 **30**   3. 34.87 **35**   4. 42.575 **43**

5. 15.91 **16**   6. 78.612 **79**   7. 4.32 **4**   8. 53.937 **54**

9. 7.4344 **7**   10. 53.409 **53**   11. 4.98 **5**   12. 1.19 **1**

Round each decimal to the nearest tenth.

1. 1.53 **1.5**   2. 1.4578 **1.5**   3. 32.277 **32.3**   4. 3.545 **3.5**

5. 2.708 **2.7**   6. 342.38 **342.4**   7. 33.897 **33.9**   8. 11.343 **11.3**

9. 3.869 **3.9**   10. 111.111 **111.1**   11. 414.74 **414.7**   12. 41.564 **41.6**

Round each decimal to the nearest hundredth.

1. 218.455 **218.46**   2. 21.564 **21.56**   3. 2.6323 **2.63**   4. 241.565 **241.57**

5. 5.5555 **5.56**   6. 212.635 **212.64**   7. 430.234 **430.23**   8. 12.1212 **12.12**

9. 12.7639 **12.76**   10. 129.414 **129.41**   11. 6.435 **6.44**   12. 7.34127 **7.34**

CD-104315 • © Carson-Dellosa   19

Name _____ Date _____

Decimals

Multiplying and Dividing by Powers of 10

$12.56 \times 10 \longrightarrow 12.56 \longrightarrow 125.6$
Move the decimal point to the right one place.

$12.56 \times 100 \longrightarrow 12.56 \longrightarrow 1256$
Move the decimal point to the right two places.

$12.565 \times 1000 \longrightarrow 12.565 \longrightarrow 12565$
Move the decimal point to the right three places.

$125.6 \div 1000 \longrightarrow 125.6 \longrightarrow 0.1256$
Move the decimal point to the left three places.

Solve each problem. Show your work.

1. $78 \times 100 =$ **7,800**
2. $0.042 \div 100 =$ **0.00042**
3. $2.7 \times 10 =$ **27**
4. $0.00198 \div 100 =$ **0.0000198**
5. $2.7453 \times 1000 =$ **2,745.3**
6. $3.581 \div 100,000 =$ **0.00003581**
7. $5123.23 \div 10,000 =$ **0.512323**
8. $2.755 \times 10 =$ **27.55**
9. $57,450 \div 100 =$ **574.5**
10. $0.0442 \times 100,000 =$ **4,420**
11. $0.000999 \times 1,000 =$ **0.999**
12. $4.342 \times 100,000 =$ **434200**
13. $67.009 \div 1000 =$ **0.067009**
14. $40,750 \times 1000 =$ **40,750,000**
15. $3.456 \times 10 =$ **34.56**
16. $345.682 \div 100 =$ **3.45682**
17. $32.949 \times 100 =$ **3294.9**
18. $35.98 \times 10,000 =$ **359,800**
19. $0.51 \div 10,000 =$ **0.000051**
20. $23,098 \div 10,000 =$ **2.3098**

20   CD-104315 • © Carson-Dellosa

Name _____ Date _____

Decimals

Adding Decimals

$12.2 + 5.25 = \begin{array}{r} 12.20 \\ + 5.25 \\ \hline 17.45 \end{array}$

Solve each problem.

1. $9.87 + 2.87 =$ **12.74**
2. $5.02 + 8.2 =$ **13.22**
3. $2.49 + 4.73 =$ **7.22**
4. $6.41 + 2.734 + 8.41 =$ **17.554**
5. $2.934 + 231.6 =$ **234.534**
6. $121.9 + 0.736 =$ **122.636**
7. $43.56 + 85.7 =$ **129.26**
8. $13.238 + 4.82 =$ **18.058**
9. $15.76 + 25.23 + 3.9 =$ **44.89**
10. $6.41 + 3.99 =$ **10.4**
11. $6.3 + 9.124 + 2.34 =$ **17.764**
12. $5.97 + 4.87 + 3.908 =$ **14.748**
13. $13.39 + 7.4 =$ **20.79**
14. $4.63 + 23.5 + 5.0 =$ **33.13**
15. $3.456 + 2.894 =$ **6.35**
16. $3.64 + 5.32 =$ **8.96**
17. $5.7 + 5.34 + 4.78 =$ **15.82**
18. $3.5 + 8.4 =$ **11.9**
19. $0.034 + 10.51 =$ **10.544**
20. $123.415 + 6.876 =$ **130.291**

CD-104315 • © Carson-Dellosa   21

Name _____ Date _____

Decimals

Adding Decimals

$7.5 + 6.12 = \begin{array}{r} 7.50 \\ + 6.12 \\ \hline 13.62 \end{array}$

Solve each problem.

1. $40.14 + 12.53 + 5.6 =$ **58.27**
2. $3.43 + 5.45 =$ **8.88**
3. $3.59 + 2.08 =$ **5.67**
4. $17.34 + 6.45 =$ **23.79**
5. $2.15 + 4.25 =$ **6.4**
6. $108.7 + 0.489 =$ **109.189**
7. $31.71 + 324.95 =$ **356.66**
8. $121.356 + 80.52 =$ **201.876**
9. $5.37 + 7.37 =$ **12.74**
10. $7.22 + 3.41 =$ **10.63**
11. $2.6 + 45.54 + 3.65 =$ **51.79**
12. $6.29 + 8.83 + 6.332 =$ **21.452**
13. $5.4 + 7.38 + 6.21 =$ **18.99**
14. $8.45 + 23.20 + 5.34 =$ **36.99**
15. $5.44 + 3.34 + 6.30 =$ **15.08**
16. $2.312 + 5.371 =$ **7.683**
17. $12.52 + 8.32 =$ **20.84**
18. $321.595 + 3.45 =$ **325.045**
19. $0.012 + 25.08 =$ **25.092**
20. $17.121 + 5.34 =$ **22.461**

22   CD-104315 • © Carson-Dellosa

Name _____ Date _____

Decimals

Subtracting Decimals

$13.2 - 4.10 = \begin{array}{r} 13.20 \\ - 4.10 \\ \hline 9.10 \end{array}$

Solve each problem.

1. $4.239 - 0.06 =$ **4.179**
2. $51.23 - 14.45 =$ **36.78**
3. $16.3 - 12.4 =$ **3.9**
4. $452.82 - 127.36 =$ **325.46**
5. $62.1 - 33.29 =$ **28.81**
6. $75.034 - 22.439 =$ **52.595**
7. $76.34 - 47.30 =$ **29.04**
8. $34.32 - 12.43 =$ **21.89**
9. $435.34 - 345.34 =$ **90**
10. $756.98 - 32.43 =$ **724.55**
11. $513.43 - 305.342 =$ **208.088**
12. $65.9 - 33.2 =$ **32.7**
13. $21.73 - 16.43 =$ **5.3**
14. $121.32 - 19.34 =$ **101.98**
15. $23.28 - 0.552 - 1.2 =$ **21.528**
16. $8.64 - 0.476 =$ **8.164**
17. $13.2 - 6.7 =$ **6.5**
18. $21.32 - 4.28 =$ **17.04**
19. $35.63 - 0.021 =$ **35.609**
20. $485.02 - 332.86 =$ **152.16**

CD-104315 • © Carson-Dellosa   23

Name _____ Date _____

Decimals

Subtracting Decimals

10.5 − 3.21 =   10.50
                − 3.21
                 7.29

Solve each problem.

1. 43,289.56 − 28,125.87 = **15,163.69**   2. 756.84 − 31.343 = **725.497**

3. 34.34 − 23.19 = **11.15**   4. 4.7 − 2.3 = **2.4**

5. 95.87 − 52.45 = **43.42**   6. 72.72 − 43.562 = **29.158**

7. 85.76 − 34.65 = **51.11**   8. 7.435 − 0.0345 = **7.4005**

9. 345.24 − 159.24 = **186**   10. 54.68 − 23.76 = **30.92**

11. 74.71 − 61.92 = **12.79**   12. 84.8 − 44.87 = **39.93**

13. 857.44 − 22.39 = **835.05**   14. 93.76 − 8.67 = **85.09**

15. 233.23 − 6.45 = **226.78**   16. 6.56 − 0.654 = **5.906**

17. 43.5 − 0.015 − 3.2 = **40.285**   18. 39.43 − 15.34 = **24.09**

19. 56.4 − 0.043 = **56.357**   20. 954.34 − 657.56 = **296.78**

24   CD-104315 • © Carson-Dellosa

Name _____ Date _____

Decimals

Multiplying Decimals

(0.3)(0.12)   0.3
                            × 0.12
3 decimal places   →   0.036

Solve each problem. Show your work.

1. (0.6)(0.022) = **0.0132**   2. (0.012)(0.7) = **0.0084**

3. (3.2)(0.65) = **2.08**   4. 0.07 × 0.4 = **0.028**

5. (0.02)(1.2) = **0.024**   6. 0.03 × 0.7 = **0.021**

7. (0.5)(0.2) = **0.1**   8. (2.2)(0.22) = **0.484**

9. (0.12)(0.04) = **0.0048**   10. 0.06 × 0.07 = **0.0042**

11. (0.11)(0.07) = **0.0077**   12. (0.13)(0.02) = **0.0026**

13. (0.7)(0.07) = **0.049**   14. (0.5)(0.05) = **0.025**

15. 0.5 × 0.06 = **0.03**   16. (0.012)(1.2) = **0.0144**

17. (0.8)(0.005) = **0.004**   18. 0.25 × 0.07 = **0.0175**

19. (0.9)(0.002) = **0.0018**   20. (0.9)(0.9) = **0.81**

CD-104315 • © Carson-Dellosa   25

Name _____ Date _____

Decimals

Multiplying Decimals Using a Calculator

Solve each problem. Use a calculator.

1. (12.3)(5.81)(0.06) = **4.28778**   2. (0.042)(0.006) = **0.000252**

3. (0.34)(0.12)(0.104) = **0.0042432**   4. (8.9)(0.11)(3.09) = **3.02511**

5. (15.92)(0.4)(0.32) = **2.03776**   6. (0.004)(6) = **0.024**

7. (6.4)(0.3) = **1.92**   8. (0.4)(0.232) = **0.0928**

9. (5.12)(6) = **30.72**   10. (10.89)(0.221) = **2.40669**

11. (3.28)(12.8) = **41.984**   12. (0.004)(0.0004)(0.04) = **0.000000064**

13. (0.016)(3.8) = **0.0608**   14. (0.007)(0.6)(0.05) = **0.00021**

15. (3.806)(10.01) = **38.09806**   16. (340)(0.02) = **6.8**

17. (0.8)(0.342)(0.02) = **0.005472**   18. (2.09)(0.005) = **0.01045**

19. (0.05)(0.15)(0.002) = **0.000015**   20. (5.4)(0.645)(0.07) = **0.24381**

21. (0.7)(0.8) = **0.56**   22. (9)(0.03)(0.2) = **0.054**

26   CD-104315 • © Carson-Dellosa

Name _____ Date _____

Decimals

Dividing Decimals

Solve each problem. Use mental math.

1. 0.036 ÷ 0.6 = **0.06**   2. 0.55 ÷ 0.005 = **110**

3. 7.2 ÷ 1.2 = **6**   4. 100 ÷ 0.01 = **10000**

5. 4.8 ÷ 0.06 = **80**   6. 0.0027 ÷ 0.9 = **0.003**

7. 1.69 ÷ 0.13 = **13**   8. 0.108 ÷ 0.09 = **1.2**

9. 0.44 ÷ 0.4 = **1.1**   10. 1.21 ÷ .11 = **11**

11. 8.4 ÷ 0.12 = **70**   12. 0.064 ÷ 0.8 = **0.08**

13. 3.6 ÷ 0.009 = **400**   14. 0.0054 ÷ 0.006 = **0.9**

15. 0.012 ÷ 0.3 = **0.04**   16. 14.4 ÷ 1.2 = **12**

17. 0.56 ÷ 0.008 = **70**   18. 2.6 ÷ 0.02 = **130**

19. 0.072 ÷ 0.08 = **0.9**   20. 6.3 ÷ 0.06 = **105**

21. 0.32 ÷ 0.008 = **40**   22. 0.132 ÷ 0.012 = **11**

CD-104315 • © Carson-Dellosa   27

Answer Key

Page 28

Name _____ Date _____

Decimals

Dividing Decimals Using a Calculator

Solve each problem. Use a calculator.

1. 6.3056 ÷ 4.2 = **1.5013̄**   2. 7.57 ÷ 0.1 = **75.7**

3. 3.56 ÷ 2.5 = **1.424**   4. 0.493 ÷ 0.33 = **1.4̄9̄3̄**

5. 8.565 ÷ 2 = **4.2825**   6. 0.0135 ÷ 4.5 = **0.003**

7. 40.78 ÷ 0.2 = **203.9**   8. 9.51 ÷ 3.03 = **3.1̄386**

9. 12.63 ÷ 0.9 = **14.03̄**   10. 9.414 ÷ 3.3 = **2.852̄7̄**

11. 1.35 ÷ 0.07 = **19.285714̄**   12. 16.73 ÷ 0.12 = **139.416̄**

13. 3.605 ÷ 3.2 = **1.1265625**   14. 0.1827 ÷ 0.09 = **2.03**

15. 12.264 ÷ 5.6 = **2.19**   16. 6.65 ÷ 2.4 = **2.77083̄**

17. 2.34 ÷ 0.012 = **195**   18. 0.576 ÷ 4.1 = **0.1404878̄**

19. 15.8 ÷ 0.09 = **175.5̄**   20. 8.176 ÷ 3.2 = **2.555**

21. 0.0224 ÷ 3.6 = **0.0062̄**   22. 21.5 ÷ 0.05 = **430**

28   CD-104315 • © Carson-Dellosa

Page 29

Name _____ Date _____

Decimals

Mixed Practice with Decimals

Solve each problem.

1. 725.987 − 231.155 = **494.832**   2. 2.34 ÷ 1.6 = **1.4625**

3. 42.25 + 53.5 = **95.75**   4. 2.62 ÷ 0.54 = **4.8̄5̄1̄**

5. (7.8)(1.03) = **8.034**   6. 23.65 ÷ 22.5 = **1.051̄**

7. 872.6 ÷ 2.4 = **363.583̄**   8. 12.828 + 10.548 = **23.376**

9. 1.32 ÷ 1.8 = **0.73̄**   10. 0.6 + 0.09 + 1.75 = **2.44**

11. 5.2 ÷ 1.2 = **4.3̄**   12. 87.21 − 13.98 + 22.23 = **95.46**

13. 13.58 − 7.2 = **6.38**   14. 432.42 − 327.89 = **104.53**

15. (3.2)(3.065) = **9.808**   16. (12.2)(34.9) = **425.78**

17. 1,343.32 − 1,032.90 = **310.42**   18. (0.04)(0.24)(1.4) = **0.01344**

19. 65.78 + 54.90 = **120.68**   20. 21.7 − 15.9 = **5.8**

21. (2.5)(3.3)(.33) = **2.7225**   22. 6.77 + 0.05 = **6.82**

CD-104315 • © Carson-Dellosa   29

Page 30

Name _____ Date _____

Decimals

Mixed Practice with Decimals

Solve each problem.

1. 3.6 ÷ 0.3 = **12**   2. 15.54 − 11.56 + 33.43 = **37.41**

3. 20.59 + 44.5 = **65.09**   4. (1.3)(3.04)(5.46) = **21.57792**

5. (4.3)(3.59) = **15.437**   6. 44.34 ÷ 32.76 = **1.3534798̄**

7. 34.96 ÷ 3.549 = **9.850662158**   8. 4.33 ÷ 0.3 = **14.4̄3̄**

9. 7.569 ÷ 3.459 = **2.188204683**   10. 154.34 + 42.98 = **197.32**

11. 17.546 + 5.0958 = **22.6418**   12. 843.21 − 452.03 = **391.18**

13. 15.51 − 8.34 = **7.17**   14. 23.565 + 28.403 = **51.968**

15. (5.5)(4.304) = **23.672**   16. 545.825 − 137.405 = **408.42**

17. 43.5 − 14.2 = **29.3**   18. (23.4)(3.9) = **91.26**

19. 0.8 + 0.07 + 3.73 = **4.6**   20. 1,350.65 − 253.42 = **1,097.23**

21. (5.5)(2.6)(4.0) = **57.2**   22. 8.37 ÷ 4.50 = **1.86**

30   CD-104315 • © Carson-Dellosa

Page 31

Name _____ Date _____

Decimals

Problem Solving with Decimals

John and Jason went to a grocery store and bought some sandwiches for $4.95, a gallon of fruit juice for $3.31, and a bag of carrots for $3.15. How much did they spend altogether?

$4.95 + $3.31 + $3.15 = $4.95
$3.31   each grocery item
+ $3.15
$11.41   total

Solve each problem. Show your work.

1. George went to the store to buy a pair of pants. The pair of pants that George picked out cost $45.00. If the price of the pants was reduced by $10.85, how much will George pay?

$34.15

2. Gary spent $13.41 on clothes in January, $25.95 in February, and $31.50 in March. Altogether, how much money did he spend on clothes in these months?

$70.86

3. Jesse buys a shirt for $32.95 and a pair of shoes for $46.25. How much money does Jesse spend in all?

$79.20

4. Heather bought some new fishing equipment. She bought a tackle box for $24.95, a fishing pole for $58.49, a life jacket for $37.75, and an ice chest for $57.41. How much money did Heather spend on her equipment?

$178.60

5. Marisol and Kurt are making sandwiches. The ingredients for the sandwiches cost $6.07. The sandwiches from the store cost $8.55. How much money are they saving?

$2.48

6. Cindy buys a shirt for $26.70, a pair of jeans for $47.55, a jacket for $25.54, and a hat for $20.11. How much does Cindy spend in all?

$119.90

CD-104315 • © Carson-Dellosa   31

110   CD-104315 • © Carson-Dellosa

Answer Key

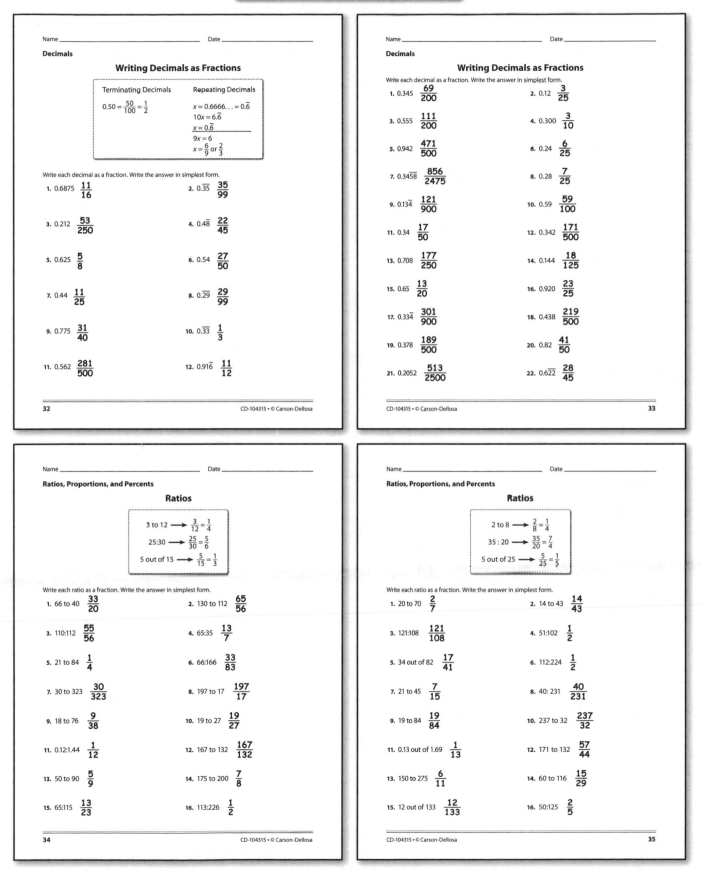

Decimals

Writing Decimals as Fractions

Terminating Decimals	Repeating Decimals
$0.50 = \frac{50}{100} = \frac{1}{2}$	$x = 0.6666\ldots = 0.\overline{6}$
	$10x = 6.\overline{6}$
	$\underline{x = 0.\overline{6}}$
	$9x = 6$
	$x = \frac{6}{9}$ or $\frac{2}{3}$

Write each decimal as a fraction. Write the answer in simplest form.

1. 0.6875 $\frac{11}{16}$
2. $0.\overline{35}$ $\frac{35}{99}$
3. 0.212 $\frac{53}{250}$
4. $0.4\overline{8}$ $\frac{22}{45}$
5. 0.625 $\frac{5}{8}$
6. 0.54 $\frac{27}{50}$
7. 0.44 $\frac{11}{25}$
8. $0.\overline{29}$ $\frac{29}{99}$
9. 0.775 $\frac{31}{40}$
10. $0.\overline{33}$ $\frac{1}{3}$
11. 0.562 $\frac{281}{500}$
12. $0.91\overline{6}$ $\frac{11}{12}$

CD-104315 • © Carson-Dellosa

Decimals

Writing Decimals as Fractions

Write each decimal as a fraction. Write the answer in simplest form.

1. 0.345 $\frac{69}{200}$
2. 0.12 $\frac{3}{25}$
3. 0.555 $\frac{111}{200}$
4. 0.300 $\frac{3}{10}$
5. 0.942 $\frac{471}{500}$
6. 0.24 $\frac{6}{25}$
7. $0.34\overline{58}$ $\frac{856}{2475}$
8. 0.28 $\frac{7}{25}$
9. $0.13\overline{4}$ $\frac{121}{900}$
10. 0.59 $\frac{59}{100}$
11. 0.34 $\frac{17}{50}$
12. 0.342 $\frac{171}{500}$
13. 0.708 $\frac{177}{250}$
14. 0.144 $\frac{18}{125}$
15. 0.65 $\frac{13}{20}$
16. 0.920 $\frac{23}{25}$
17. $0.33\overline{4}$ $\frac{301}{900}$
18. 0.438 $\frac{219}{500}$
19. 0.378 $\frac{189}{500}$
20. 0.82 $\frac{41}{50}$
21. 0.2052 $\frac{513}{2500}$
22. $0.6\overline{22}$ $\frac{28}{45}$

CD-104315 • © Carson-Dellosa

Ratios, Proportions, and Percents

Ratios

3 to 12 → $\frac{3}{12} = \frac{1}{4}$
25:30 → $\frac{25}{30} = \frac{5}{6}$
5 out of 15 → $\frac{5}{15} = \frac{1}{3}$

Write each ratio as a fraction. Write the answer in simplest form.

1. 66 to 40 $\frac{33}{20}$
2. 130 to 112 $\frac{65}{56}$
3. 110:112 $\frac{55}{56}$
4. 65:35 $\frac{13}{7}$
5. 21 to 84 $\frac{1}{4}$
6. 66:166 $\frac{33}{83}$
7. 30 to 323 $\frac{30}{323}$
8. 197 to 17 $\frac{197}{17}$
9. 18 to 76 $\frac{9}{38}$
10. 19 to 27 $\frac{19}{27}$
11. 0.12:1.44 $\frac{1}{12}$
12. 167 to 132 $\frac{167}{132}$
13. 50 to 90 $\frac{5}{9}$
14. 175 to 200 $\frac{7}{8}$
15. 65:115 $\frac{13}{23}$
16. 113:226 $\frac{1}{2}$

CD-104315 • © Carson-Dellosa

Ratios, Proportions, and Percents

Ratios

2 to 8 → $\frac{2}{8} = \frac{1}{4}$
35 : 20 → $\frac{35}{20} = \frac{7}{4}$
5 out of 25 → $\frac{5}{25} = \frac{1}{5}$

Write each ratio as a fraction. Write the answer in simplest form.

1. 20 to 70 $\frac{2}{7}$
2. 14 to 43 $\frac{14}{43}$
3. 121:108 $\frac{121}{108}$
4. 51:102 $\frac{1}{2}$
5. 34 out of 82 $\frac{17}{41}$
6. 112:224 $\frac{1}{2}$
7. 21 to 45 $\frac{7}{15}$
8. 40: 231 $\frac{40}{231}$
9. 19 to 84 $\frac{19}{84}$
10. 237 to 32 $\frac{237}{32}$
11. 0.13 out of 1.69 $\frac{1}{13}$
12. 171 to 132 $\frac{57}{44}$
13. 150 to 275 $\frac{6}{11}$
14. 60 to 116 $\frac{15}{29}$
15. 12 out of 133 $\frac{12}{133}$
16. 50:125 $\frac{2}{5}$

CD-104315 • © Carson-Dellosa

Proportions

Name _____ Date _____

Ratios, Proportions, and Percents

$$\frac{2}{6} = \frac{x}{18}$$
$$2 \cdot 18 = 6x$$
$$\frac{36}{6} = \frac{6x}{6}$$
$$6 = x$$

Solve each proportion. Use cross–products.

1. $\frac{1}{4} = \frac{x}{8}$ **2**   2. $\frac{20}{30} = \frac{5}{x}$ **$7\frac{1}{2}$**

3. $\frac{18}{24} = \frac{12}{x}$ **16**   4. $\frac{80}{x} = \frac{48}{20}$ **$33\frac{1}{3}$**

5. $\frac{5}{5} = \frac{5x}{5}$ **1**   6. $\frac{15}{45} = \frac{3}{x}$ **9**

7. $\frac{1.8}{x} = \frac{3.6}{2.8}$ **1.4**   8. $\frac{8}{x} = \frac{5}{2}$ **$3\frac{1}{5}$**

9. $\frac{8}{6} = \frac{x}{27}$ **36**   10. $\frac{144}{6} = \frac{6x}{6}$ **24**

11. $\frac{x}{3} = \frac{8}{8}$ **3**   12. $\frac{36}{12} = \frac{x}{6}$ **18**

13. $\frac{0.14}{0.07} = \frac{x}{1.5}$ **3**   14. $\frac{6}{x} = \frac{6}{4}$ **4**

15. $\frac{4}{5} = \frac{x}{5}$ **4**   16. $\frac{16}{48} = \frac{x}{50}$ **$16\frac{2}{3}$**

Problem Solving with Proportions

Name _____ Date _____

Ratios, Proportions, and Percents

If 3 liters of juice cost $3.75, how much does 9 liters cost?

$$\frac{\text{liters}}{\text{cost}} = \frac{3}{3.75} = \frac{9}{x}$$
$$3x = 3.75 \cdot 9$$
$$\frac{3x}{3} = \frac{33.75}{3} \qquad x = 11.25$$
9 liters cost $11.25

Solve each problem. Round each answer to the nearest cent.

1. If 3 square feet of fabric cost $3.75, what would 7 square feet cost?

$8.75

2. A 12-ounce bottle of soap costs $2.50. How many ounces would be in a bottle that costs $3.75?

18 ounces

3. Four pounds of apples cost $5.00. How much would 10 pounds of apples cost?

$12.50

4. A 12-ounce can of lemonade costs $1.32. How much would a 16-ounce can of lemonade cost?

$1.76

5. J & S Jewelry company bought 800 bracelets for $450.00. How much did each bracelet cost?

$1.78

6. A dozen peaches costs $3.60. How much did each peach cost?

$0.30

7. A 32-pound box of cantaloupe costs $24.40. How much would a 12-pound box cost?

$9.15

8. If a 10-pound turkey costs $20.42, how much would a 21-pound turkey cost?

$42.88

Percents

Name _____ Date _____

Ratios, Proportions, and Percents

Fraction to percent	Decimal to percent
$\frac{1}{2} \longrightarrow \frac{1}{2} = \frac{x}{100}$	$0.425 \longrightarrow 0.425 = 42.5\%$
$2x = 100$	When converting a decimal
$x = 50$	to a percent, move the decimal
$\frac{1}{2} = 50\%$	two places to the right.

Write each fraction or decimal as a percent. Round each answer to the nearest hundredth.

1. $\frac{7}{21}$ **33.33%**   2. 10.8 **1080%**

3. 12.392 **1239.2%**   4. 523.32 **52332%**

5. 2.3839 **238.39%**   6. $\frac{12}{19}$ **63.16%**

7. $\frac{5}{46}$ **10.87%**   8. $\frac{11}{23}$ **47.83%**

9. $\frac{4}{13}$ **30.77%**   10. 2.32 **232%**

11. 17.45 **1745%**   12. 5.293 **529.3%**

Percents

Name _____ Date _____

Ratios, Proportions, and Percents

$$60\% = \frac{60}{100} = \frac{6}{10} = \frac{3}{5}$$
$$51.5\% = \frac{51.5}{100} = \frac{515}{1,000} = \frac{103}{200}$$

Write each percent as a fraction. Write each fraction as a percent. Write the answers that are fractions in simplest form.

1. 0.68% **$\frac{17}{2,500}$**   2. 33.8% **$\frac{169}{500}$**

3. 8.6% **$\frac{43}{500}$**   4. 21.98% **$\frac{1,099}{5,000}$**

5. 4.934% **$\frac{2,467}{50,000}$**   6. $7\frac{4}{21}$ **719.05%**

7. 5.75% **$\frac{23}{400}$**   8. $3\frac{34}{88}$ **338.64%**

9. $4\frac{5}{46}$ **410.87%**   10. $2\frac{5}{7}$ **271.43%**

11. 364.69% **$\frac{36469}{10000}$**   12. $21\frac{7}{32}$ **2,121.88%**

13. 12.4% **$\frac{31}{250}$**   14. $6\frac{1}{2}$ **650%**

15. $1\frac{3}{4}$ **175%**   16. 2.98% **$\frac{149}{5,000}$**

Name _____ Date _____

Ratios, Proportions, and Percents

Percents

50% of 60 = ____	____% of 40 = 20	40% of ____ = 30
$\frac{50}{100} = \frac{x}{60}$	$\frac{x}{100} = \frac{20}{40}$	$\frac{40}{100} = \frac{30}{x}$
$100x = 3000$	$40x = 2000$	$40x = 3000$
$x = 30$	$x = 50$ 50%	$x = 75$

Solve each problem.

1. 20% of 15 = **3**

2. 30% of 60 = **18**

3. 15% of 75 = **11.25**

4. 37% of 65 = **24.05**

5. 44% of 40 = **17.6**

6. ____% of 35 = 15 **42.86%**

7. ____% of 70 = 20 **28.57%**

8. ____% of 48 = 8 **16.6%**

9. ____% of 65 = 33 **50.77%**

10. ____% of 9 = 4 **44.4%**

11. 12% of ____ = 76 **633.3**

12. 65% of ____ = 80 **123.08**

13. 20% of ____ = 75 **375**

14. 45% of ____ = 150 **333.3**

15. 22% of ____ = 34 **154.54**

16. 50% of ____ = 52 **104**

Name _____ Date _____

Ratios, Proportions, and Percents

Problem Solving with Percents

A baseball team played 30 games and won 50% of them. How many games did the team win?
50% of 30 = ____
$\frac{50}{100} = \frac{x}{30}$
$100x = 1500$
$x = 15$ games

Solve each problem. Show your work.

1. In a group of 35 students, 7 have yellow socks. What percentage of the students have yellow socks?

    20%

2. A test has 60 questions. Fred answers 75% of them correctly. How many problems does Fred answer correctly?

    45 answers

3. A football team plays 25 games. They win 32% of them. How many games does the team win?

    8 games

4. The regular price of a pair of pants is $38.00. The pants are discounted 35%. How much do the pants cost after the discount is applied?

    $24.70

5. A store was having a sale on books. The book Bart wants is priced at $19.00. He has a coupon for 30% off. How much does the book cost after the coupn is applied?

    $13.30

6. Lisa went to a restaurant and gave the waiter a 15% tip. If the price of her meal was $10.25, how much did Lisa tip the waiter?

    $1.54

7. Emily bought a new car that cost $22,000. The car was 93% of the list price. How much was the list price?

    $23,655.91

Name _____ Date _____

Integers

Adding Integers with Like Signs

$5 + 5 = 10$ (positive)	$(^-3) + (^-10) = ^-13$ (negative)
2 positives	2 negatives

Solve each problem.

1. $(^-13) + (^-34) + (^-67) =$ **$^-114$**

2. $90 + 52 =$ **142**

3. $(^-12) + (^-7) =$ **$^-19$**

4. $5 + 6 =$ **11**

5. $32 + 53 =$ **85**

6. $23 + 54 + 56 =$ **133**

7. $(^-34) + (^-76) =$ **$^-110$**

8. $142 + 374 =$ **516**

9. $(^-42) + (^-36) + (^-22) =$ **$^-100$**

10. $13 + 45 + 84 =$ **142**

11. $(^-35) + (^-38) =$ **$^-73$**

12. $45 + 8 =$ **53**

13. $(^-16) + (^-16) + (^-16) =$ **$^-48$**

14. $15 + 41 + 7 =$ **63**

15. $(^-60) + (^-39) =$ **$^-99$**

16. $(^-2) + (^-124) + (^-438) =$ **$^-564$**

17. $(^-12) + (^-34) + (^-46) + (^-261) =$ **$^-353$**

18. $12 + 45 + 332 =$ **389**

19. $(^-16) + (^-16) =$ **$^-32$**

20. $23 + 72 =$ **95**

Name _____ Date _____

Integers

Adding Integers with Like Signs

$6 + 6 = 12$ (positive)	$(^-3) + (^-4) = ^-7$ (negative)
2 positives	2 negatives

Solve each problem.

1. $(^-21) + (^-22) + (^-41) =$ **$^-84$**

2. $50 + 82 =$ **132**

3. $(^-14) + (^-9) =$ **$^-23$**

4. $7 + 8 =$ **15**

5. $27 + 53 =$ **80**

6. $50 + 63 + 82 =$ **195**

7. $(^-21) + (^-34) =$ **$^-55$**

8. $36 + 57 + 58 =$ **151**

9. $213 + 375 =$ **588**

10. $(^-21) + (^-41) + (^-55) =$ **$^-117$**

11. $(^-163) + (^-238) =$ **$^-401$**

12. $(^-14) + (^-34) + (^-67) =$ **$^-115$**

13. $(^-23) + (^-48) =$ **$^-71$**

14. $(^-21) + (^-59) + (^-828) =$ **$^-908$**

15. $29 + 67 =$ **96**

16. $21 + 22 + 23 =$ **66**

17. $34 + 46 =$ **80**

18. $(^-13) + (^-65) + (^-78) + (^-332) =$ **$^-488$**

19. $(^-20) + (^-68) =$ **$^-88$**

20. $51 + 87 + 527 =$ **665**

Name _____ Date _____

Integers

Adding Integers with Unlike Signs

$5 + (-13) = -8$ $\qquad$ $-12 + 14 = 2$
$5 - 13 = -8$ $\qquad$ $14 - 12 = 2$

Solve each problem.

1. $8 + (-11) =$ **-3**

2. $-73 + 12 =$ **-61**

3. $-17 + 6 =$ **-11**

4. $310 + (-673) =$ **-363**

5. $56 + (-7) =$ **49**

6. $-1,565 + 576 =$ **-989**

7. $-17 + 33 =$ **16**

8. $17,985 + (-22,581) =$ **-4,596**

9. $-213 + 56 =$ **-157**

10. $-563,937 + 76,412 =$ **-487,525**

11. $-167 + 121 =$ **-46**

12. $-12 + 9 =$ **-3**

13. $48 + (-56) =$ **-8**

14. $45,908 + (-12,921) =$ **32,987**

15. $-61 + 61 =$ **0**

16. $-19 + 39 =$ **20**

17. $-34,132 + 81,323 =$ **47,191**

18. $57 + (-90) =$ **-33**

19. $34 + (-34) =$ **0**

20. $642 + (-423) =$ **219**

44 $\qquad$ CD-104315 • © Carson-Dellosa

Name _____ Date _____

Integers

Adding Integers with Unlike Signs

$4 + (-12) = -8$ $\qquad$ $-10 + 14 = 4$
$4 - 12 = -8$ $\qquad$ $14 - 10 = 4$

Solve each problem.

1. $24 + (-67) =$ **-43**

2. $-6,607 + 4,362 =$ **-2,245**

3. $-194 + 635 =$ **441**

4. $-23,895 + 5,863 =$ **-18,032**

5. $321 + (-494) =$ **-173**

6. $714 + (-6,976) =$ **-6,262**

7. $-43 + 68 =$ **25**

8. $131,985 + (-454,202) =$ **-322,217**

9. $-343 + 439 =$ **96**

10. $-112,956 + 564,258 =$ **451,302**

11. $-595 + 630 =$ **35**

12. $67,888 + (-78,952) =$ **-11,064**

13. $55,980 + (-42,278) =$ **13,702**

14. $-64,412 + 73,651 =$ **9,239**

15. $-99 + 94 =$ **-5**

16. $88 + (-34) =$ **54**

17. $-84,154 + 89,343 =$ **5,189**

18. $34,139 + (-56,913) =$ **-22,774**

19. $-73 + 25 =$ **-48**

20. $850 + (-828) =$ **22**

CD-104315 • © Carson-Dellosa $\qquad$ 45

Name _____ Date _____

Integers

Subtracting Integers

$6 - 10 = 6 + (-10) = -4$ $\qquad$ $6 - (-10) = 6 + 10 = 16$
Add the opposite $\qquad$ Add the opposite

Solve each problem.

1. $-8 - 3 =$ **-11**

2. $56 - (-65) =$ **121**

3. $-52 - (-34) =$ **-18**

4. $-19 - (-13) =$ **-6**

5. $42 - 23 =$ **19**

6. $77 - 22 =$ **55**

7. $17 - 26 =$ **-9**

8. $-594 - (-73) =$ **-521**

9. $-117 - 29 =$ **-146**

10. $-749 - 629 =$ **-1,378**

11. $19 - (-342) =$ **361**

12. $2,567 - (-492) =$ **3,059**

13. $5,762 - 2,144 =$ **3,618**

14. $121 - 154 =$ **-33**

15. $-8 - (-27) =$ **19**

16. $-87 - 129 =$ **-216**

17. $45 - 75 =$ **-30**

18. $688 - 456 =$ **232**

19. $187 - (-48) =$ **235**

20. $157 - (-452) =$ **609**

46 $\qquad$ CD-104315 • © Carson-Dellosa

Name _____ Date _____

Integers

Subtracting Integers

Solve each problem.

1. $7 - 15 =$ **-8**

2. $319 - (-749) =$ **1,068**

3. $-18 - 6 =$ **-24**

4. $-60 - 17 =$ **-77**

5. $-45 - (-45) =$ **0**

6. $-54 - (-95) =$ **41**

7. $-154 - 56 =$ **-210**

8. $-625 - 127 =$ **-752**

9. $-21 - (-45) =$ **24**

10. $564 - (-373) =$ **937**

11. $3 - (-67) =$ **70**

12. $6,593 - (-4,132) =$ **10,725**

13. $0 - 15 =$ **-15**

14. $108,762 - (-95,671) =$ **204,433**

15. $-3 - (-7) =$ **4**

16. $-9,774 - 8,834 =$ **-18,608**

17. $-5 - (-67) =$ **62**

18. $-23 - 56 =$ **-79**

19. $-44 - 57 =$ **-101**

20. $-475,824 - (-153,198) =$ **-322,626**

21. $-36 - 69 =$ **-105**

22. $-934 - (-672) =$ **-262**

23. $-630,805 - (-512,156) =$ **-118,649**

24. $899,342 - (-392,231) =$ **1,291,573**

CD-104315 • © Carson-Dellosa $\qquad$ 47

Name _____ Date _____

Integers

Adding and Subtracting Integers

Solve each problem.

1. ⁻233 – (⁻233) = **0**
2. ⁻16 – (⁻38) = **22**
3. ⁻19 – 4 = **⁻23**
4. 0 – 17 = **⁻17**
5. ⁻13 + 26 = **13**
6. ⁻59 – 43 = **⁻102**
7. 31 – (⁻8) = **39**
8. 43 + (⁻56) – 78 = **⁻91**
9. ⁻16 + 9 = **⁻7**
10. ⁻8 + (⁻5) = **⁻13**
11. ⁻9 – (⁻24) = **15**
12. ⁻103 + (⁻575) = **⁻678**
13. ⁻78 – 65 = **⁻143**
14. 71 + (⁻18) = **53**
15. 12 + (⁻7) = **5**
16. 0 – (⁻9) = **9**
17. 109 – (⁻53) = **162**
18. 91 – 157 – (⁻33) = **⁻33**
19. ⁻129 + ⁻645 – (⁻13) = **⁻761**
20. ⁻17 + 436 + (⁻642) = **⁻223**
21. ⁻534 – (⁻454) + (⁻58) = **⁻138**
22. ⁻98 – (⁻126) + 19 = **47**
23. 509 – 343 = **166**
24. 24 + (⁻64) = **⁻40**

Name _____ Date _____

Integers

Multiplying Integers

(3)(3) = 9	(⁻2)(⁻3) = 6	(⁻3)(3) = ⁻9	(⁻2)(3) = ⁻6
Like signs = Positive		Unlike signs = Negative	

Solve each problem.

1. (33)(⁻123)(12) = **⁻48,708**
2. (⁻434)(⁻7) = **3,038**
3. (15)(⁻4) = **⁻60**
4. (⁻5)(⁻28)(⁻23) = **⁻3,220**
5. (30)(5) = **150**
6. (13)(⁻28) = **⁻364**
7. (⁻72)(43) = **⁻3,096**
8. (⁻3)(9) = **⁻27**
9. (56)(12) = **672**
10. (14)(⁻33)(2) = **⁻924**
11. (32)(⁻48) = **⁻1,536**
12. (20)(⁻3)(23)(⁻3) = **4,140**
13. (⁻39)(⁻58) = **2,262**
14. (12)(⁻12)(2)(⁻33) = **9,504**
15. (⁻20)(⁻10)(2)(3) = **1,200**
16. (37)(⁻90) = **⁻3,330**
17. (121)(⁻10)(21) = **⁻25,410**
18. (⁻9)(⁻88)(⁻7) = **⁻5,544**
19. (⁻13)(⁻13) = **169**
20. (⁻32)(⁻22)(⁻45) = **⁻31,680**

Name _____ Date _____

Integers

Multiplying Integers

(3)(4) = 12	(⁻3)(⁻5) = 15	(⁻3)(2) = ⁻6	(⁻2)(5) = ⁻10
Like signs = Positive		Unlike signs = Negative	

Solve each problem.

1. (8)(⁻99)(⁻22)(⁻7) = **⁻121,968**
2. (⁻9)(⁻82)(⁻7) = **⁻5,166**
3. (⁻7)(3) = **⁻21**
4. (⁻6)(⁻9) = **54**
5. (⁻10)(⁻5)(⁻3) = **⁻150**
6. (5)(⁻4)(⁻3) = **60**
7. (⁻7)(⁻2)(⁻5) = **⁻70**
8. (⁻7)(⁻14)(144) = **14,112**
9. (⁻17)(⁻2) = **34**
10. (⁻2)(⁻13)(⁻4) = **⁻104**
11. (⁻8)(⁻9) = **72**
12. (⁻1)(22)(⁻33)(44) = **31,944**
13. (21)(⁻22) = **⁻462**
14. (⁻85)(⁻215) = **18,275**
15. (4)(111)(⁻1) = **⁻444**
16. (213)(4)(18) = **15,336**
17. (⁻19)(⁻38) = **722**
18. (⁻5)(⁻100)(⁻302) = **⁻151,000**
19. (1)(⁻41)(⁻6) = **246**
20. (⁻33)(213) = **⁻7,029**

Name _____ Date _____

Integers

Dividing Integers

$\frac{-18}{-3}$ = 6	24 ÷ (⁻4) = ⁻6
Like signs = Positive	Unlike signs = Negative

Solve each problem.

1. 100 ÷ (⁻4) = **⁻25**
2. $\frac{-18}{10}$ = **⁻1**
3. ⁻60 ÷ 3 = **⁻20**
4. $\frac{-104}{8}$ = **⁻13**
5. 120 ÷ (⁻6) = **⁻20**
6. $\frac{-77}{7}$ = **⁻11**
7. 88 ÷ (⁻22) = **⁻4**
8. $\frac{36}{-9}$ = **⁻4**
9. ⁻188 ÷ 4 = **⁻47**
10. $\frac{168}{21}$ = **8**
11. 144 ÷ (⁻12) = **⁻12**
12. $\frac{-50}{-5}$ = **10**
13. 80 ÷ (⁻5) = **⁻16**
14. ⁻36 ÷ 6 = **⁻6**
15. 72 ÷ 4 = **18**
16. $\frac{169}{-13}$ = **⁻13**
17. $\frac{210}{-10}$ = **⁻21**
18. $\frac{-50}{-5}$ = **10**
19. ⁻150 ÷ 6 = **⁻25**
20. $\frac{-288}{-12}$ = **24**

Name _____ Date _____

Integers

Dividing Integers

Solve each problem.

1. $^-14 \div 14 =$ **$^-1$**

2. $\frac{^-77}{11} =$ **$^-7$**

3. $60 \div (^-10) =$ **$^-6$**

4. $^-160 \div (^-40) =$ **4**

5. $^-72 \div 9 =$ **$^-8$**

6. $\frac{^-80}{10} =$ **$^-8$**

7. $\frac{^-755}{^-5} =$ **151**

8. $\frac{^-72}{8} =$ **$^-9$**

9. $^-54 \div (^-9) =$ **6**

10. $\frac{^-35}{^-7} =$ **5**

11. $^-195 \div (^-65) =$ **3**

12. $\frac{^-468}{26} =$ **$^-18$**

13. $^-150 \div (^-50) =$ **3**

14. $\frac{^-253}{11} =$ **$^-23$**

15. $189 \div (^-21) =$ **$^-9$**

16. $\frac{66}{^-2} =$ **$^-33$**

17. $75 \div (^-3) =$ **$^-25$**

18. $\frac{^-84}{^-7} =$ **12**

19. $^-210 \div (^-5) =$ **42**

20. $\frac{^-552}{^-23} =$ **24**

21. $^-94 \div 2 =$ **$^-47$**

22. $\frac{^-310}{5} =$ **$^-62$**

23. $^-125 \div 5 =$ **$^-25$**

24. $\frac{^-258}{^-3} =$ **86**

Name _____ Date _____

Integers

Mixed Practice with Integers

Solve each problem.

1. $(625 \div 5) \times 0.2 =$ **25**

2. $\frac{150}{(^-5)} \times (^-4) =$ **120**

3. $80 - (^-22) =$ **102**

4. $\frac{^-555}{(^-5)} \times (^-6) =$ **$^-666$**

5. $^-3 \times 5 =$ **$^-15$**

6. $\frac{^-424}{4} =$ **$^-106$**

7. $19 - 23 =$ **$^-4$**

8. $(\frac{^-72}{9}) + (\frac{^-64}{8}) + (\frac{44}{^-11}) =$ **$^-20$**

9. $83 + (^-85) =$ **$^-2$**

10. $(^-34) + (^-255) =$ **$^-289$**

11. $28 - (^-65) =$ **93**

12. $28 - (^-26) =$ **54**

13. $[^-19 - (^-21) - (^-34)] \div (^-6) =$ **$^-6$**

14. $[^-18 - (^-66) ^-22] \times 2 =$ **52**

15. $^-61 - (^-21) =$ **$^-40$**

16. $(16 - 21 + 34) \div (^-8) =$ **$^-3\frac{5}{8}$**

17. $^-35 + 62 + (^-80) =$ **$^-53$**

18. $[10 + (^-31) + (^-80)] \div 3 =$ **$^-33\frac{2}{3}$**

19. $(^-13 - 54 - 30) \times 2 =$ **$^-194$**

20. $[^-160 + (^-75) + 24] \times 4 =$ **$^-844$**

21. $56 \times 3 \times 21 =$ **3,528**

22. $(^-12 + 13 + 55) \div 3 =$ **$18\frac{2}{3}$**

Name _____ Date _____

Integers

Problem Solving with Integers

Solve each problem. Show your work.

1. A helicopter started out at an altitude of 0 feet. It then rose to an altitude of 2,150 feet. Then, it descended 400 feet in order to see a herd of bison. It then rose 4,200 feet in order to avoid a passing plane. After the plane passed, the helicopter descended 2,200 feet. What was the helicopter's altitude at the end?

3,750 feet

2. Julio goes to school in a 9-story building. His first class of the day is on the second floor. For his second class, Julio goes up 5 floors. For his third class, Julio goes down 1 floor. For his fourth class, Julio goes up 3 floors, and for his last class he goes down 2 floors. What floor is Julio on during his last class?

7th floor

3. Some number added to $^-12$ is 45. Add this number to 30. Multiply the answer by 3. What is the final number?

261

4. Some number multiplied by $^-6$ is 36. Multiply this number by 8. Divide the answer by 2. What is the final number?

$^-24$

5. A bus driver started her day with no passengers. Then, 13 people got on at the first stop. At the second stop, 8 people got on and 6 left the bus. At the third stop, 5 people got on and 3 left the bus. How many people are on the bus after the third stop?

17 passengers

6. The school library started the year with 9,561 books. At the end of the first week of school, 1,625 books had been checked out. At the end of the second week, 5,140 books had been checked out. By the end of two weeks 913 books had been returned. How many books were in the library at the end of the second week?

3,709 books

Name _____ Date _____

Real Numbers

Adding and Subtracting Real Numbers

$$^-4 + (^-3) + 2\frac{1}{3} = ^-7 + 2\frac{1}{3} = ^-6\frac{3}{3} + 2\frac{1}{3} = ^-4\frac{2}{3}$$

Solve each problem.

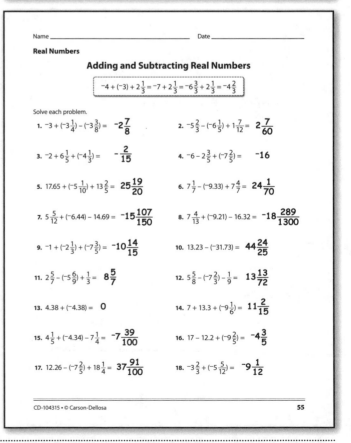

1. $^-3 + (^-3\frac{1}{4}) - (^-3\frac{3}{8}) =$ **$^-2\frac{7}{8}$**

2. $^-5\frac{2}{3} - (^-6\frac{1}{5}) + 1\frac{7}{12} =$ **$2\frac{7}{60}$**

3. $^-2 + 6\frac{1}{5} + (^-4\frac{1}{3}) =$ **$^-\frac{2}{15}$**

4. $^-6 - 2\frac{3}{5} + (^-7\frac{2}{5}) =$ **$^-16$**

5. $17.65 + (^-5\frac{1}{10}) + 13\frac{2}{5} =$ **$25\frac{19}{20}$**

6. $7\frac{1}{7} - (^-9.33) + 7\frac{4}{7} =$ **$24\frac{1}{70}$**

7. $5\frac{5}{12} + (^-6.44) - 14.69 =$ **$^-15\frac{107}{150}$**

8. $7\frac{4}{13} + (^-9.21) - 16.32 =$ **$^-18\frac{289}{1300}$**

9. $^-1 + (^-2\frac{1}{3}) + (^-7\frac{3}{5}) =$ **$^-10\frac{14}{15}$**

10. $13.23 - (^-31.73) =$ **$44\frac{24}{25}$**

11. $2\frac{5}{7} - (^-5\frac{6}{9}) + \frac{1}{3} =$ **$8\frac{5}{7}$**

12. $5\frac{5}{8} - (^-7\frac{2}{3}) - \frac{1}{9} =$ **$13\frac{13}{72}$**

13. $4.38 + (^-4.38) =$ **0**

14. $7 + 13.3 + (^-9\frac{1}{6}) =$ **$11\frac{2}{15}$**

15. $4\frac{1}{5} + (^-4.34) - 7\frac{1}{4} =$ **$^-7\frac{39}{100}$**

16. $17 - 12.2 + (^-9\frac{2}{5}) =$ **$^-4\frac{3}{5}$**

17. $12.26 - (^-7\frac{2}{5}) + 18\frac{1}{4} =$ **$37\frac{91}{100}$**

18. $^-3\frac{2}{3} + (^-5\frac{5}{12}) =$ **$^-9\frac{1}{12}$**

Real Numbers

Adding and Subtracting Real Numbers

Solve each problem.

1. $-8\frac{1}{2} + (-2\frac{4}{12}) - 8\frac{1}{3} =$ $-19\frac{1}{6}$

2. $5\frac{2}{5} + (-3.43) - 8\frac{3}{10} =$ $-6\frac{33}{100}$

3. $-6 - 7\frac{3}{4} + (-2\frac{2}{3}) =$ $-16\frac{5}{12}$

4. $-8 - 1\frac{3}{5} + (-6\frac{1}{8}) =$ $-15\frac{29}{40}$

5. $-2\frac{3}{7} + (-9\frac{6}{21}) - 5\frac{2}{3} =$ $-17\frac{8}{21}$

6. $3\frac{2}{5} + (-2.25) - 7\frac{2}{4} =$ $-6\frac{7}{20}$

7. $6\frac{1}{10} + (-3.25) - 12.65 =$ $-9\frac{4}{5}$

8. $-11.08 - (-12.67) =$ $1\frac{59}{100}$

9. $-2 - (-3\frac{1}{8}) + (-4\frac{3}{4}) =$ $-3\frac{5}{8}$

10. $17 - 12.2 - (-8\frac{4}{9}) =$ $13\frac{11}{45}$

11. $6\frac{2}{3} - (-1\frac{2}{3}) + \frac{2}{3} =$ 9

12. $3\frac{1}{2} - (-6\frac{1}{3}) - \frac{3}{5} =$ $9\frac{7}{30}$

13. $12 - 15.3 + (-7\frac{2}{3}) =$ $-10\frac{29}{30}$

14. $-5 - (-7\frac{3}{7}) + (-2\frac{5}{8}) =$ $-\frac{11}{56}$

15. $3\frac{1}{15} + (-4.38) - 13.47 =$ $-14\frac{47}{60}$

16. $-5.23 + 3.33 =$ $-1\frac{9}{10}$

17. $14.33 - (-5\frac{3}{4}) + 13\frac{2}{3} =$ $33\frac{56}{75}$

18. $17\frac{8}{9} - 12.2 + 16\frac{2}{7} =$ $21\frac{307}{315}$

19. $5\frac{2}{3} - (-5.61) - 8\frac{1}{5} =$ $3\frac{23}{300}$

20. $11.62 + (-8\frac{6}{7}) - \frac{18}{9} =$ $\frac{267}{350}$

21. $3\frac{7}{10} + (-4.23) - 7\frac{3}{8} =$ $-7\frac{181}{200}$

22. $11\frac{2}{5} - 17.8 + 13\frac{4}{5} =$ $7\frac{2}{5}$

Real Numbers

Multiplying and Dividing Real Numbers

$$2 \times 3 \times \frac{1}{2} = 6 \times \frac{1}{2} = \frac{6}{1} \times \frac{1}{2} = 3$$
$$2\frac{1}{2} \times 1\frac{3}{4} \div 1\frac{1}{2} = \frac{5}{2} \times \frac{7}{4} \div \frac{3}{2} = \frac{5}{2} \times \frac{7}{4} \times \frac{2}{3} = \frac{35}{12} = 2\frac{11}{12}$$

Solve each problem.

1. $2\frac{1}{3} \div 1\frac{1}{2} \times \frac{5}{6} =$ $1\frac{8}{27}$

2. $2\frac{1}{7} \div (-5.56) =$ $-\frac{375}{973}$

3. $-3 \times 2\frac{1}{5} \times (-7\frac{1}{3}) =$ $48\frac{2}{5}$

4. $7 \div 2.5 \times (-3\frac{2}{5}) =$ $-9\frac{13}{25}$

5. $-8\frac{2}{3} \times 3\frac{7}{15} =$ $-30\frac{2}{45}$

6. $5\frac{1}{3} \times 9.80 \times 0 =$ 0

7. $1\frac{5}{12} \times 3.29 =$ $4\frac{793}{1200}$

8. $11 \times 3\frac{1}{12} \times (-3) =$ $-101\frac{3}{4}$

9. $7 \times (-2\frac{1}{3}) \times 2 =$ $-32\frac{2}{3}$

10. $(-3\frac{1}{4})(-3\frac{1}{4}) \div 2 =$ $5\frac{9}{32}$

11. $5\frac{1}{2} \div (-3\frac{1}{6}) =$ $-1\frac{14}{19}$

12. $2\frac{2}{3} \times (-6\frac{1}{5}) =$ $-16\frac{8}{15}$

13. $-6.3 \times 2 \times \frac{1}{2} =$ $-6\frac{3}{10}$

14. $10 \div 12.1 \div (-6\frac{1}{6}) =$ $-\frac{600}{4,477}$

15. $9.21 \times (-7\frac{1}{3}) \div 25\frac{5}{9} =$ -2.643

16. $6.21 \times (-1.37) =$ -8.5077

17. $10.6 \div (-2\frac{1}{2}) \times 3\frac{1}{4} =$ $-13\frac{39}{50}$

18. $3.6 \times (-31.72) =$ -114.192

Real Numbers

Multiplying and Dividing Real Numbers

Solve each problem.

1. $6\frac{1}{5} \times 3.55 \times 0 =$ 0

2. $5\frac{1}{3} \div (-3.84) =$ $-1\frac{7}{18}$

3. $-6 \times 8\frac{2}{8} \times (-1\frac{1}{4}) =$ $61\frac{7}{8}$

4. $13 \times 5\frac{1}{10} \times (-2) =$ $-132\frac{3}{5}$

5. $-5\frac{1}{6} \times 2\frac{7}{18} =$ $-12\frac{37}{108}$

6. $1\frac{1}{14} \div (-3\frac{2}{7}) =$ $-\frac{15}{46}$

7. $3\frac{3}{8} \times 2.27 =$ $7\frac{529}{800}$

8. $-2.2 \times 5 \times \frac{1}{7} =$ $-1\frac{4}{7}$

9. $2 \times (-1\frac{1}{2}) \times 6 =$ -18

10. $10 \div 2.5 \times (-4\frac{4}{7}) =$ $-18\frac{2}{7}$

11. $5.25 \times (-3.89) =$ -20.4225

12. $2\frac{1}{5} \div 6\frac{3}{7} \div \frac{4}{6} =$ $\frac{77}{150}$

13. $(-7\frac{2}{8})(-3\frac{2}{8}) \div 0.2 =$ $117\frac{13}{16}$

14. $8.10 \times (-5\frac{1}{6}) \div 15\frac{5}{6} =$ $-2\frac{611}{950}$

15. $4.2 \times (-12.12) =$ -50.904

16. $3\frac{2}{3} \div (-6\frac{1}{5}) =$ $-\frac{55}{93}$

17. $12.2 \times (-6\frac{1}{5}) \times 3\frac{2}{5} =$ $-257\frac{22}{125}$

18. $12.12 \times (-12\frac{2}{6}) \div 12\frac{1}{3} =$ $-12\frac{3}{25}$

19. $13.5 \div (-3\frac{2}{3}) \times 6\frac{3}{7} =$ $-23\frac{103}{154}$

20. $12 \times 12.3 \times (-6\frac{1}{2}) =$ $-959\frac{2}{5}$

21. $12.8 \times (-5\frac{2}{3}) \times 2\frac{4}{5} =$ $-203\frac{7}{75}$

22. $13.26 \times (-8\frac{1}{3}) \div 12\frac{5}{7} =$ $-8\frac{123}{178}$

Real Numbers

Order of Operations with Real Numbers

$$-4 \times 2 + 2 = -8 + 2 = -6$$
$$2\frac{1}{4} \div (4 + 8) = \frac{9}{8} \div 12 = \frac{9}{8} \times \frac{1}{12} = \frac{9}{96} \text{ or } \frac{3}{32}$$

Solve each problem. Use the order of operations rules.

1. $2 \times 3 [7 + (6 \div 2)] =$ 60

2. $\frac{2}{3}(-15 - 4) =$ $-12\frac{2}{3}$

3. $-8 \div (-2) + 5 \times (\frac{-1}{2}) - 25 \div 5 =$ $-3\frac{1}{2}$

4. $-30 \div 6 + 4\frac{1}{5} =$ $-\frac{4}{5}$

5. $(9\frac{1}{3} + 4\frac{1}{3}) \div 6 - (-12) =$ $14\frac{5}{18}$

6. $\frac{[(60 \div 4) + 35]}{(-12 + 35)} =$ $2\frac{4}{23}$

7. $\frac{3}{4} [(-15 + 4) + (6 + 7) \div (-3)] =$ $-11\frac{1}{2}$

8. $3[-3(2 - 8) - 6] =$ 36

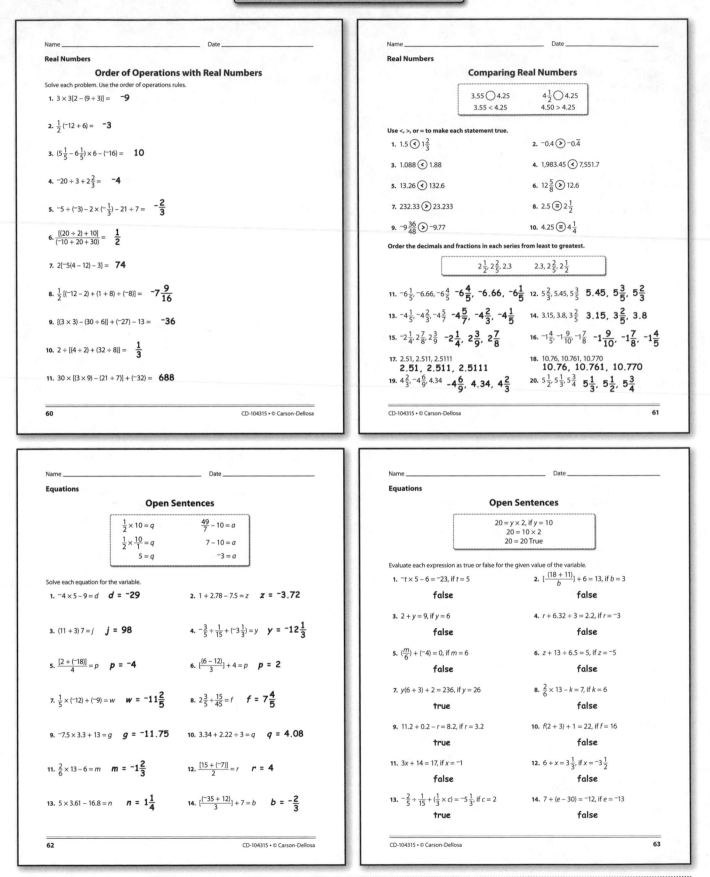

Name _____ Date _____

Real Numbers

Order of Operations with Real Numbers

Solve each problem. Use the order of operations rules.

1. $3 \times 3[2 - (9 \div 3)] =$ **-9**

2. $\frac{1}{2}(-12 + 6) =$ **-3**

3. $(5\frac{1}{5} - 6\frac{1}{5}) \times 6 - (-16) =$ **10**

4. $-20 \div 3 + 2\frac{2}{3} =$ **-4**

5. $-5 \div (-3) - 2 \times (-\frac{1}{3}) - 21 \div 7 =$ **$-\frac{2}{3}$**

6. $\frac{[(20 \div 2) + 10]}{(-10 + 20 + 30)} =$ **$\frac{1}{2}$**

7. $2[-5(4 - 12) - 3] =$ **74**

8. $\frac{1}{2}[(-12 - 2) + (1 + 8) \div (-8)] =$ **$-7\frac{9}{16}$**

9. $[(3 \times 3) - (30 \div 6)] + (-27) - 13 =$ **-36**

10. $2 \div [(4 \div 2) + (32 \div 8)] =$ **$\frac{1}{3}$**

11. $30 \times [(3 \times 9) - (21 \div 7)] + (-32) =$ **688**

60 CD-104315 • © Carson-Dellosa

Name _____ Date _____

Real Numbers

Comparing Real Numbers

$3.55 \bigcirc 4.25$ $4\frac{1}{2} \bigcirc 4.25$
$3.55 < 4.25$ $4.50 > 4.25$

Use <, >, or = to make each statement true.

1. $1.5 \, \textcircled{<} \, 1\frac{2}{3}$

2. $-0.4 \, \textcircled{>} \, -0.\overline{4}$

3. $1.088 \, \textcircled{<} \, 1.88$

4. $1,983.45 \, \textcircled{<} \, 7,551.7$

5. $13.26 \, \textcircled{<} \, 132.6$

6. $12\frac{5}{8} \, \textcircled{>} \, 12.6$

7. $232.33 \, \textcircled{>} \, 23.233$

8. $2.5 \, \textcircled{=} \, 2\frac{1}{2}$

9. $-9\frac{36}{48} \, \textcircled{>} \, -9.77$

10. $4.25 \, \textcircled{=} \, 4\frac{1}{4}$

Order the decimals and fractions in each series from least to greatest.

$2\frac{1}{2}, 2\frac{2}{5}, 2.3$ $2.3, 2\frac{2}{5}, 2\frac{1}{2}$

11. $-6\frac{1}{5}, -6.66, -6\frac{4}{5}$ **$-6\frac{4}{5}, -6.66, -6\frac{1}{5}$**

12. $5\frac{2}{3}, 5.45, 5\frac{3}{5}$ **$5.45, 5\frac{3}{5}, 5\frac{2}{3}$**

13. $-4\frac{1}{5}, -4\frac{2}{3}, -4\frac{5}{7}$ **$-4\frac{5}{7}, -4\frac{2}{3}, -4\frac{1}{5}$**

14. $3.15, 3.8, 3\frac{2}{5}$ **$3.15, 3\frac{2}{5}, 3.8$**

15. $-2\frac{1}{4}, 2\frac{7}{8}, 2\frac{3}{9}$ **$-2\frac{1}{4}, 2\frac{3}{9}, 2\frac{7}{8}$**

16. $-1\frac{4}{5}, -1\frac{9}{10}, -1\frac{7}{8}$ **$-1\frac{9}{10}, -1\frac{7}{8}, -1\frac{4}{5}$**

17. $2.51, 2.511, 2.5111$ **$2.51, 2.511, 2.5111$**

18. $10.76, 10.761, 10.770$ **$10.76, 10.761, 10.770$**

19. $4\frac{2}{3}, -4\frac{6}{9}, 4.34$ **$-4\frac{6}{9}, 4.34, 4\frac{2}{3}$**

20. $5\frac{1}{2}, 5\frac{1}{3}, 5\frac{3}{4}$ **$5\frac{1}{3}, 5\frac{1}{2}, 5\frac{3}{4}$**

CD-104315 • © Carson-Dellosa 61

Name _____ Date _____

Equations

Open Sentences

$\frac{1}{2} \times 10 = q$ $\frac{49}{7} - 10 = a$
$\frac{1}{2} \times \frac{10}{1} = q$ $7 - 10 = a$
$5 = q$ $-3 = a$

Solve each equation for the variable.

1. $-4 \times 5 - 9 = d$ **$d = -29$**

2. $1 + 2.78 - 7.5 = z$ **$z = -3.72$**

3. $(11 + 3) \, 7 = j$ **$j = 98$**

4. $-\frac{3}{5} \div \frac{1}{15} + (-3\frac{1}{3}) = y$ **$y = -12\frac{1}{3}$**

5. $\frac{[2 + (-18)]}{4} = p$ **$p = -4$**

6. $[\frac{(6 - 12)}{3}] + 4 = p$ **$p = 2$**

7. $\frac{1}{5} \times (-12) + (-9) = w$ **$w = -11\frac{2}{5}$**

8. $2\frac{3}{5} \div \frac{15}{45} = f$ **$f = 7\frac{4}{5}$**

9. $-7.5 \times 3.3 + 13 = g$ **$g = -11.75$**

10. $3.34 + 2.22 \div 3 = q$ **$q = 4.08$**

11. $\frac{2}{6} \times 13 - 6 = m$ **$m = -1\frac{2}{3}$**

12. $\frac{[15 + (-7)]}{2} = r$ **$r = 4$**

13. $5 \times 3.61 - 16.8 = n$ **$n = 1\frac{1}{4}$**

14. $[\frac{(-35 + 12)}{3}] + 7 = b$ **$b = -\frac{2}{3}$**

62 CD-104315 • © Carson-Dellosa

Name _____ Date _____

Equations

Open Sentences

$20 = y \times 2$, if $y = 10$
$20 = 10 \times 2$
$20 = 20$ True

Evaluate each expression as true or false for the given value of the variable.

1. $-t \times 5 - 6 = -23$, if $t = 5$ **false**

2. $[\frac{(18 + 11)}{b}] + 6 = 13$, if $b = 3$ **false**

3. $2 + y = 9$, if $y = 6$ **false**

4. $r + 6.32 \div 3 = 2.2$, if $r = -3$ **false**

5. $(\frac{m}{6}) + (-4) = 0$, if $m = 6$ **false**

6. $z + 13 \div 6.5 = 5$, if $z = -5$ **false**

7. $y(6 + 3) + 2 = 236$, if $y = 26$ **true**

8. $\frac{2}{6} \times 13 - k = 7$, if $k = 6$ **false**

9. $11.2 + 0.2 - r = 8.2$, if $r = 3.2$ **true**

10. $f(2 + 3) + 1 = 22$, if $f = 16$ **false**

11. $3x + 14 = 17$, if $x = -1$ **false**

12. $6 + x = 3\frac{1}{3}$, if $x = -3\frac{1}{2}$ **false**

13. $-\frac{2}{5} \div \frac{1}{15} + (\frac{1}{3} \times c) = -5\frac{1}{3}$, if $c = 2$ **true**

14. $7 + (e - 30) = -12$, if $e = -13$ **false**

CD-104315 • © Carson-Dellosa 63

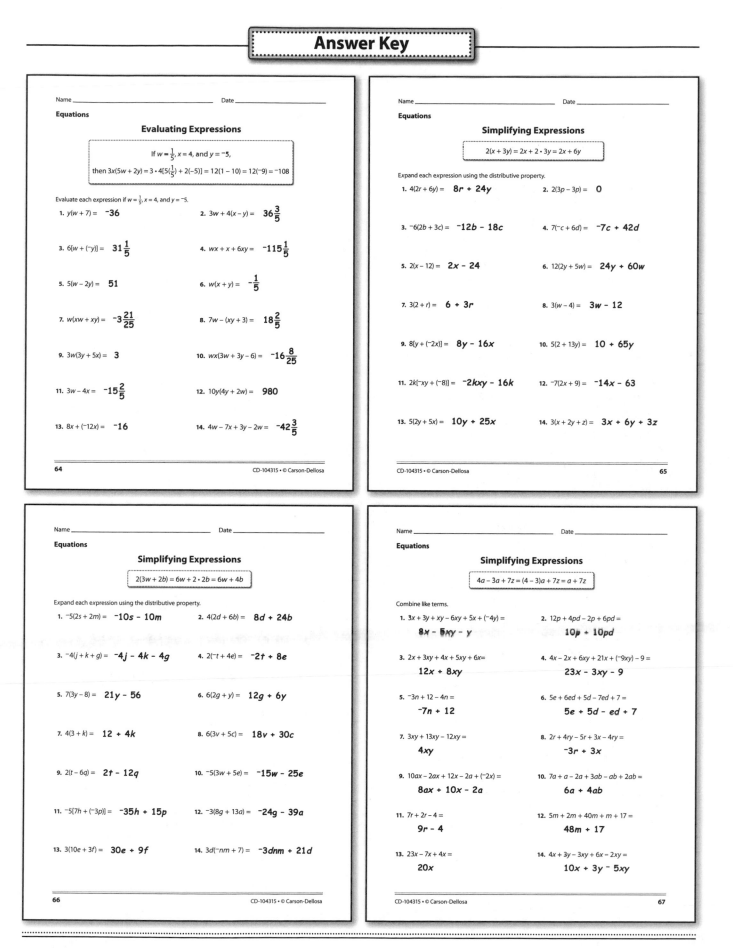

Name _____ Date _____

Equations

Evaluating Expressions

If $w = \frac{1}{5}$, $x = 4$, and $y = ^-5$,

then $3x(5w + 2y) = 3 \cdot 4[5(\frac{1}{5}) + 2(^-5)] = 12(1 - 10) = 12(^-9) = ^-108$

Evaluate each expression if $w = \frac{1}{5}$, $x = 4$, and $y = ^-5$.

1. $y(w + 7) =$ **$^-36$**

2. $3w + 4(x - y) =$ **$36\frac{3}{5}$**

3. $6[w + (^-y)] =$ **$31\frac{1}{5}$**

4. $wx + x + 6xy =$ **$^-115\frac{1}{5}$**

5. $5(w - 2y) =$ **51**

6. $w(x + y) =$ **$^-\frac{1}{5}$**

7. $w(xw + xy) =$ **$^-3\frac{21}{25}$**

8. $7w - (xy + 3) =$ **$18\frac{2}{5}$**

9. $3w(3y + 5x) =$ **3**

10. $wx(3w + 3y - 6) =$ **$^-16\frac{8}{25}$**

11. $3w - 4x =$ **$^-15\frac{2}{5}$**

12. $10y(4y + 2w) =$ **980**

13. $8x + (^-12x) =$ **$^-16$**

14. $4w - 7x + 3y - 2w =$ **$^-42\frac{3}{5}$**

64   CD-104315 • © Carson-Dellosa

Name _____ Date _____

Equations

Simplifying Expressions

$2(x + 3y) = 2x + 2 \cdot 3y = 2x + 6y$

Expand each expression using the distributive property.

1. $4(2r + 6y) =$ **$8r + 24y$**

2. $2(3p - 3p) =$ **0**

3. $^-6(2b + 3c) =$ **$^-12b - 18c$**

4. $7(^-c + 6d) =$ **$^-7c + 42d$**

5. $2(x - 12) =$ **$2x - 24$**

6. $12(2y + 5w) =$ **$24y + 60w$**

7. $3(2 + r) =$ **$6 + 3r$**

8. $3(w - 4) =$ **$3w - 12$**

9. $8[y + (^-2x)] =$ **$8y - 16x$**

10. $5(2 + 13y) =$ **$10 + 65y$**

11. $2k[^-xy + (^-8)] =$ **$^-2kxy - 16k$**

12. $^-7(2x + 9) =$ **$^-14x - 63$**

13. $5(2y + 5x) =$ **$10y + 25x$**

14. $3(x + 2y + z) =$ **$3x + 6y + 3z$**

CD-104315 • © Carson-Dellosa   65

Name _____ Date _____

Equations

Simplifying Expressions

$2(3w + 2b) = 6w + 2 \cdot 2b = 6w + 4b$

Expand each expression using the distributive property.

1. $^-5(2s + 2m) =$ **$^-10s - 10m$**

2. $4(2d + 6b) =$ **$8d + 24b$**

3. $^-4(j + k + g) =$ **$^-4j - 4k - 4g$**

4. $2(^-t + 4e) =$ **$^-2t + 8e$**

5. $7(3y - 8) =$ **$21y - 56$**

6. $6(2g + y) =$ **$12g + 6y$**

7. $4(3 + k) =$ **$12 + 4k$**

8. $6(3v + 5c) =$ **$18v + 30c$**

9. $2(t - 6q) =$ **$2t - 12q$**

10. $^-5(3w + 5e) =$ **$^-15w - 25e$**

11. $^-5[7h + (^-3p)] =$ **$^-35h + 15p$**

12. $^-3(8g + 13a) =$ **$^-24g - 39a$**

13. $3(10e + 3f) =$ **$30e + 9f$**

14. $3d(^-nm + 7) =$ **$^-3dnm + 21d$**

66   CD-104315 • © Carson-Dellosa

Name _____ Date _____

Equations

Simplifying Expressions

$4a - 3a + 7z = (4 - 3)a + 7z = a + 7z$

Combine like terms.

1. $3x + 3y + xy - 6xy + 5x + (^-4y) =$ **$8x - 5xy - y$**

2. $12p + 4pd - 2p + 6pd =$ **$10p + 10pd$**

3. $2x + 3xy + 4x + 5xy + 6x=$ **$12x + 8xy$**

4. $4x - 2 + 6xy + 21x + (^-9xy) - 9 =$ **$23x - 3xy - 9$**

5. $^-3n + 12 - 4n =$ **$^-7n + 12$**

6. $5e + 6ed + 5d - 7ed + 7 =$ **$5e + 5d - ed + 7$**

7. $3xy + 13xy - 12xy =$ **$4xy$**

8. $2r + 4ry - 5r + 3x - 4ry =$ **$^-3r + 3x$**

9. $10ax - 2ax + 12x - 2a + (^-2x) =$ **$8ax + 10x - 2a$**

10. $7a + a - 2a + 3ab - ab + 2ab =$ **$6a + 4ab$**

11. $7r + 2r - 4 =$ **$9r - 4$**

12. $5m + 2m + 40m + m + 17 =$ **$48m + 17$**

13. $23x - 7x + 4x =$ **$20x$**

14. $4x + 3y - 3xy + 6x - 2xy =$ **$10x + 3y - 5xy$**

CD-104315 • © Carson-Dellosa   67

Name _____ Date _____

Equations

Simplifying Expressions

$$5g - 3g + 2h = (5 - 3)g + 2h = 2g + 2h$$

Combine like terms.

1. $7(2x + 5y) + 6xy - 6(3xy + 5x) =$
$-16x - 12xy + 35y$

2. $10p + 5pd - 2p + 6pd =$
$8p + 11pd$

3. $9x - 4x + 2x + 8(6x + 2x) =$
$71x$

4. $3(x - 5x) + 2(xy + 7x) + (^-7xy) =$
$2x - 5xy$

5. $3c - 4bc + (^-7b) + 3[2bc - (^-b)] =$
$3c + 2bc - 4b$

6. $^-2a - [^-3(a + 7)] - 4(^-a + b) =$
$5a + 21 - 4b$

7. $2t + 12t - 4(n + 4n) =$
$14t - 20n$

8. $6r + 5r - 8p + 6p + 7(2r - 4r) =$
$^-3r - 2p$

9. $3n(x - y) + 3n(x + y) - 2 =$
$6nx - 2$

10. $3[h - (^-k)] + 2[^-3h + (^-4k)] =$
$^-3h - 5k$

11. $^-2(g + 5g) + ^-2[6f - (^-12g)] =$
$^-12f - 36g$

12. $4(2x + 2y) - 2[3xy - (^-5x)] =$
$^-2x + 8y - 6xy$

13. $5m + 3mn - (^-9n) + 2(m - n) =$
$3mn + 7m + 7n$

14. $5xy - 12xy + 12xy - 9(x + y) =$
$5xy - 9x - 9y$

68   CD-104315 • © Carson-Dellosa

Name _____ Date _____

Equations

Solving Addition Equations

$$1.4 = ^-2.4 + x$$
$$1.4 + 2.4 = ^-2.4 + 2.4 + x$$
$$3.8 = 0 + x$$
$$3.8 = x$$

Solve each equation for the variable.

1. $x + (^-5\frac{3}{4}) = ^-10\frac{1}{4}$ **$x = ^-4\frac{1}{2}$**

2. $^-35 = x + 35$ **$x = ^-70$**

3. $w + 79 = ^-95$ **$w = ^-174$**

4. $^-\frac{1}{4} + x = ^-\frac{1}{4}$ **$x = 0$**

5. $7 + c = ^-14$ **$c = ^-21$**

6. $^-4.5 = 9\frac{1}{2} + c$ **$c = ^-14$**

7. $^-21 = t + 18$ **$t = ^-39$**

8. $22 = c + (^-13)$ **$c = 35$**

9. $^-9 + r = 22$ **$r = 31$**

10. $x + (^-8) = 9$ **$x = 17$**

11. $3.5 = n + 4.6$ **$n = ^-1.1$**

12. $^-2\frac{1}{2} + k = ^-3\frac{5}{7}$ **$k = ^-1\frac{3}{14}$**

13. $^-2,929 + t = 4,242$ **$t = 7,171$**

14. $z + 5.2 = 7.1$ **$z = 1.9$**

CD-104315 • © Carson-Dellosa   69

Name _____ Date _____

Equations

Solving Subtraction Equations

$$32 = x - (^-8)$$
$$32 = x + 8$$
$$32 - 8 = x + 8 - 8$$
$$24 = x + 0$$
$$24 = x$$

Solve each equation for the variable.

1. $^-2,547 = n - 5,534$ **$n = 2,987$**

2. $^-44 = m - 32$ **$m = ^-12$**

3. $t - (^-8) = 45$ **$t = 37$**

4. $^-\frac{1}{3} - g = ^-\frac{1}{3}$ **$g = 0$**

5. $^-15 = p - 6$ **$p = ^-9$**

6. $3.65 = n - 7$ **$n = 10.65$**

7. $34 = b - (^-2)$ **$b = 32$**

8. $a + (^-4\frac{1}{3}) = ^-15\frac{1}{3}$ **$a = ^-11$**

9. $f - 16 = ^-32$ **$f = ^-16$**

10. $x - 8 = 34$ **$x = 42$**

11. $^-3.4 = h - 8.5$ **$h = 5.1$**

12. $^-2.2 = 8\frac{4}{5} + d$ **$d = ^-11$**

13. $^-3\frac{2}{3} + k = ^-6\frac{3}{4}$ **$k = 3\frac{1}{12}$**

14. $z - (^-21.5) = ^-2.356$ **$z = ^-23.856$**

70   CD-104315 • © Carson-Dellosa

Name _____ Date _____

Equations

Solving Addition and Subtraction Equations

$$10 = c - 8$$
$$10 + 8 = c - 8 + 8$$
$$18 = c + 0$$
$$18 = c$$

Solve each equation for the variable.

1. $^-\frac{3}{4} + j = ^-3\frac{1}{2}$ **$j = ^-2\frac{3}{4}$**

2. $11.4 - k = 5.2$ **$k = 6.2$**

3. $^-8\frac{3}{7} + t = ^-9\frac{2}{5}$ **$t = ^-\frac{34}{35}$**

4. $^-3.1 = 4\frac{3}{4} + e$ **$e = ^-7\frac{17}{20}$**

5. $b + (^-9) = 36$ **$b = 45$**

6. $5.77 = q + 9$ **$q = ^-3.23$**

7. $^-56 = c - (^-8)$ **$c = ^-64$**

8. $^-3,282 = n + 1,111$ **$n = ^-4,393$**

9. $t + 12 = ^-18$ **$t = ^-30$**

10. $^-6.7 = y - 27$ **$y = 20.3$**

11. $f + (^-3\frac{1}{4}) = ^-7\frac{1}{4}$ **$f = ^-4$**

12. $w - (^-43.7) = ^-3.674$ **$w = ^-47.374$**

13. $31 = u - 12$ **$u = 43$**

14. $x + 9 = ^-22$ **$x = ^-31$**

CD-104315 • © Carson-Dellosa   71

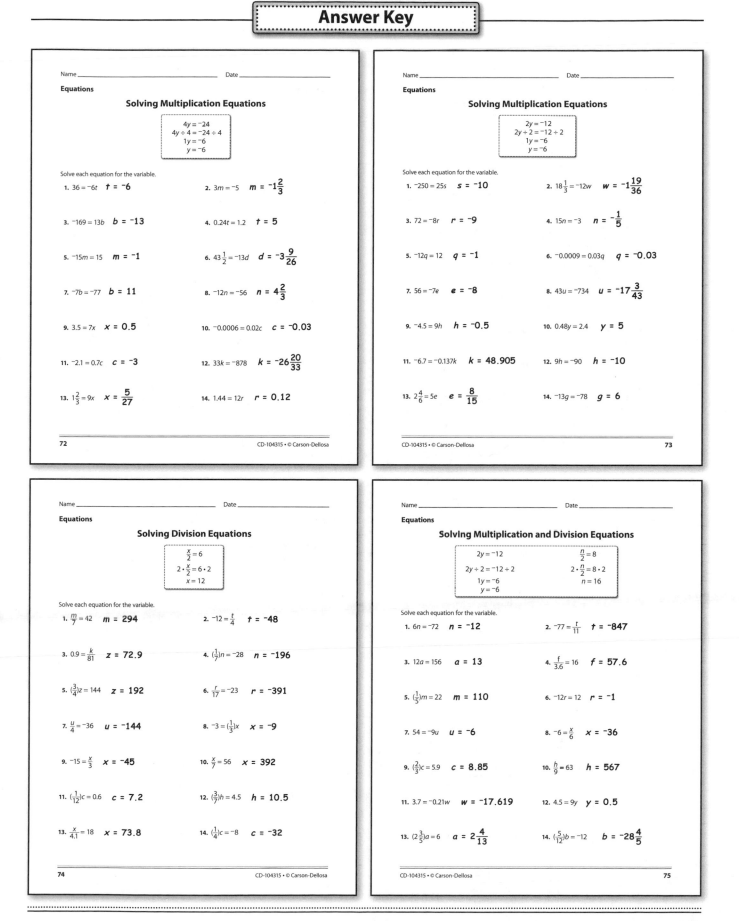

Name_____ Date_____

Equations

Solving Multiplication Equations

$$4y = ^-24$$
$$4y \div 4 = ^-24 \div 4$$
$$1y = ^-6$$
$$y = ^-6$$

Solve each equation for the variable.

1. $36 = ^-6t$ **t = ⁻6**

2. $3m = ^-5$ **m = ⁻1$\frac{2}{3}$**

3. $^-169 = 13b$ **b = ⁻13**

4. $0.24t = 1.2$ **t = 5**

5. $^-15m = 15$ **m = ⁻1**

6. $43\frac{1}{2} = ^-13d$ **d = ⁻3$\frac{9}{26}$**

7. $^-7b = ^-77$ **b = 11**

8. $^-12n = ^-56$ **n = 4$\frac{2}{3}$**

9. $3.5 = 7x$ **x = 0.5**

10. $^-0.0006 = 0.02c$ **c = ⁻0.03**

11. $^-2.1 = 0.7c$ **c = ⁻3**

12. $33k = ^-878$ **k = ⁻26$\frac{20}{33}$**

13. $1\frac{2}{3} = 9x$ **x = $\frac{5}{27}$**

14. $1.44 = 12r$ **r = 0.12**

72   CD-104315 • © Carson-Dellosa

Name_____ Date_____

Equations

Solving Multiplication Equations

$$2y = ^-12$$
$$2y \div 2 = ^-12 \div 2$$
$$1y = ^-6$$
$$y = ^-6$$

Solve each equation for the variable.

1. $^-250 = 25s$ **s = ⁻10**

2. $18\frac{1}{3} = ^-12w$ **w = ⁻1$\frac{19}{36}$**

3. $72 = ^-8r$ **r = ⁻9**

4. $15n = ^-3$ **n = ⁻$\frac{1}{5}$**

5. $^-12q = 12$ **q = ⁻1**

6. $^-0.0009 = 0.03q$ **q = ⁻0.03**

7. $56 = ^-7e$ **e = ⁻8**

8. $43u = ^-734$ **u = ⁻17$\frac{3}{43}$**

9. $^-4.5 = 9h$ **h = ⁻0.5**

10. $0.48y = 2.4$ **y = 5**

11. $^-6.7 = ^-0.137k$ **k = 48.905**

12. $9h = ^-90$ **h = ⁻10**

13. $2\frac{4}{6} = 5e$ **e = $\frac{8}{15}$**

14. $^-13g = ^-78$ **g = 6**

CD-104315 • © Carson-Dellosa   73

Name_____ Date_____

Equations

Solving Division Equations

$$\frac{x}{2} = 6$$
$$2 \cdot \frac{x}{2} = 6 \cdot 2$$
$$x = 12$$

Solve each equation for the variable.

1. $\frac{m}{7} = 42$ **m = 294**

2. $^-12 = \frac{t}{4}$ **t = ⁻48**

3. $0.9 = \frac{k}{81}$ **z = 72.9**

4. $(\frac{1}{7})n = ^-28$ **n = ⁻196**

5. $(\frac{3}{4})z = 144$ **z = 192**

6. $\frac{r}{17} = ^-23$ **r = ⁻391**

7. $\frac{u}{4} = ^-36$ **u = ⁻144**

8. $^-3 = (\frac{1}{3})x$ **x = ⁻9**

9. $^-15 = \frac{x}{3}$ **x = ⁻45**

10. $\frac{x}{7} = 56$ **x = 392**

11. $(\frac{1}{12})c = 0.6$ **c = 7.2**

12. $(\frac{3}{7})h = 4.5$ **h = 10.5**

13. $\frac{x}{4.1} = 18$ **x = 73.8**

14. $(\frac{1}{4})c = ^-8$ **c = ⁻32**

74   CD-104315 • © Carson-Dellosa

Name_____ Date_____

Equations

Solving Multiplication and Division Equations

$$2y = ^-12 \qquad \frac{n}{2} = 8$$
$$2y \div 2 = ^-12 \div 2 \qquad 2 \cdot \frac{n}{2} = 8 \cdot 2$$
$$1y = ^-6 \qquad n = 16$$
$$y = ^-6$$

Solve each equation for the variable.

1. $6n = ^-72$ **n = ⁻12**

2. $^-77 = \frac{t}{11}$ **t = ⁻847**

3. $12a = 156$ **a = 13**

4. $\frac{f}{3.6} = 16$ **f = 57.6**

5. $(\frac{1}{5})m = 22$ **m = 110**

6. $^-12r = 12$ **r = ⁻1**

7. $54 = ^-9u$ **u = ⁻6**

8. $^-6 = \frac{x}{6}$ **x = ⁻36**

9. $(\frac{2}{3})c = 5.9$ **c = 8.85**

10. $\frac{h}{9} = 63$ **h = 567**

11. $3.7 = ^-0.21w$ **w = ⁻17.619**

12. $4.5 = 9y$ **y = 0.5**

13. $(2\frac{3}{5})a = 6$ **a = 2$\frac{4}{13}$**

14. $(\frac{5}{12})b = ^-12$ **b = ⁻28$\frac{4}{5}$**

CD-104315 • © Carson-Dellosa   75

Name _____ Date _____

Equations

Solving Equations with Two Operations

$$2y - 10 = 30$$
$$2y - 10 + 10 = 30 + 10$$
$$\frac{2y}{2} = \frac{40}{2}$$
$$y = 20$$

Solve each equation for the variable. Write the answer in simplest form.

1. $14 = 6c - 4$ $c = 3$
2. $13n - 13 = -12$ $n = \frac{1}{13}$

3. $5x - 5 = -10$ $x = -1$
4. $23x - 12 = -33$ $x = -\frac{21}{23}$

5. $10 = 3y + 5$ $y = 1\frac{2}{3}$
6. $-42 = 6b + 8$ $b = -8\frac{1}{3}$

7. $-23 = 3e - (-9)$ $e = -10\frac{2}{3}$
8. $16 + 4y = -32$ $y = -12$

9. $-8r - 9 = -24$ $r = 1\frac{7}{8}$
10. $16 + \frac{r}{2} = -11$ $r = -54$

11. $12 = 3y - 12$ $y = 8$
12. $2x - 5 = 16$ $x = 10\frac{1}{2}$

13. $\frac{3y}{4} = 12$ $y = 16$
14. $16 = -2v + 9$ $v = -3\frac{1}{2}$

Name _____ Date _____

Equations

Solving Equations Using the Distributive Property

$$2(a - 3) = 14$$
$$2a - 6 = 14$$
$$2a - 6 + 6 = 14 + 6$$
$$\frac{2a}{2} = \frac{20}{2}$$
$$a = 10$$

Solve each equation for the variable.

1. $-4(6 + n) + 3 = 36$ $n = -14\frac{1}{4}$
2. $3(8 - 6n) = 42$ $n = -1$

3. $35 = -7(z + 8)$ $z = -13$
4. $2(n + 6) = 80$ $n = 34$

5. $30 = 5[(\frac{r}{5}) - 3]$ $r = 45$
6. $-23 = 5(t - 4)$ $t = -\frac{3}{5}$

7. $-7(t - 7) = -14$ $t = 9$
8. $2(9x - 8) = -22$ $x = -\frac{1}{3}$

9. $16(x - 3) = -33$ $x = \frac{15}{16}$
10. $-36 = 2(x + 4)$ $x = -22$

11. $8(2x - 4) + 4 = 24$ $x = 3\frac{1}{4}$
12. $3(c + 4) = -8$ $c = -6\frac{2}{3}$

13. $5(3 - \frac{c}{7}) = 8$ $c = 9\frac{4}{5}$
14. $36 = 6(x - 5)$ $x = 11$

Name _____ Date _____

Equations

Solving Equations

$$2x + 5 = 3x + 6$$
$$2x - 3x + 5 = 3x - 3x + 6$$
$$-x + 5 = 6$$
$$-x + 5 - 5 = 6 - 5$$
$$-x = 1$$
$$\frac{-x}{-1} = \frac{1}{-1}$$
$$x = -1$$

Solve each equation for the variable.

1. $4n - 6 = 6n + 14$ $n = -10$
2. $-6g + 12 = 2g + 12$ $g = 0$

3. $-t + 9 = t + 5$ $t = 2$
4. $23b + 9 = 4b + 66$ $b = 3$

5. $7y - 7 = 5y + 13$ $y = 10$
6. $-8t = 27 + t$ $t = -3$

7. $10w + 6 = 6w - 15$ $w = -5\frac{1}{4}$
8. $13y - 26 = 7y + 22$ $y = 8$

9. $-r - 5 = 1 - 2r$ $r = 6$
10. $3m - 8 = 5m + 8$ $m = -8$

11. $4x - 7 = 2x + 7$ $x = 7$
12. $2e + 20 = 4e - 12$ $e = 16$

13. $18 + 2p = 8p - 13$ $p = 5\frac{1}{6}$
14. $4h + 10 = 2h - 22$ $h = -16$

Name _____ Date _____

Equations

Mixed Practice with Equations

Solve each equation for the variable.

1. $-2j + 6 = 2j - 8$ $j = 3\frac{1}{2}$
2. $4h + 6 = 2h - 8$ $h = -7$

3. $9w + 9 = 3w - 15$ $w = -4$
4. $45 = -9(e + 8)$ $e = -13$

5. $35 = -7t$ $t = -5$
6. $12k + 13 = 8k + 33$ $k = 5$

7. $6u = 28 - u$ $u = 4$
8. $7(9 - 6j) = -63$ $j = 3$

9. $4(y - 8) = -12$ $y = 5$
10. $-6(36 - 10b) + 8 = 32$ $b = 4$

11. $-14k = 56$ $k = -4$
12. $9(8c - 9) = -351$ $c = -3\frac{3}{4}$

13. $11g = 121$ $g = 11$
14. $\frac{m}{2.5} = 22$ $m = 55$

15. $24 = 4[(\frac{h}{2}) - 7]$ $h = 26$
16. $-6 = \frac{b}{6}$ $b = -36$

17. $4g + 12 = 6g - 4$ $g = 8$
18. $(\frac{2}{5}) h = -20$ $h = -50$

Name _____ Date _____

Problem Solving

Writing Algebraic Expressions

Three times a number increased by 5	$3x + 5$
A number increased by 3	$x + 3$
A number divided by 2	$x \div 2$ or $\frac{x}{2}$
The product of 2 and 6	$2 \cdot 6$

Write the algebraic expression.

1. Two-fifths of a number decreased by 3 $\left(\frac{2}{5}\right)x - 3$

2. Twelve times a number decreased by 4 $12x - 4$

3. Eight times the difference between x and 7 $8(x - 7)$

4. The product of 3 and a number increased by 6 $3x + 6$

5. One-third times a number increased by 7 $\frac{1}{3}x + 7$

6. Four increased by 7 times a number $4 + 7x$

7. Seven times the sum of twice a number and 16 $7(2x + 16)$

8. Eleven times the sum of a number and 5 times the number $11(x + 5x)$

9. Five times a number plus 6 times the number $5x + 6x$

10. The quotient of a number and 5 decreased by 3 $\frac{x}{5} - 3$

11. Four times the sum of a number and 8 $4(x + 8)$

12. A number increased by 9 times the number $x + 9x$

80   CD-104315 • © Carson-Dellosa

Name _____ Date _____

Problem Solving

Writing Algebraic Expressions

Two times a number increased by 4	$2x + 4$
A number increased by 2	$x + 2$
A number divided by 4	$x \div 4$ or $\frac{x}{4}$
The product of 3 and 5	$3 \cdot 5$

Write an equation for each expression.

1. Two-thirds of a number increased by 9 $\left(\frac{2x}{3}\right) + 9$

2. The quotient of 6 and a number increased by 3 $\frac{6}{x} + 3$

3. Nine more than the quotient of b and 4 $\frac{b}{4} + 9$

4. Four-sevenths of a number minus 6 $\left(\frac{4x}{7}\right) - 6$

5. Three-fourths times a number increased by 6 $\left(\frac{3x}{4}\right) + 6$

6. Three increased by 4 times a number $3 + 4x$

7. Three times a number plus 7 times the number $3x + 7x$

8. A number increased by 9 times the number $x + 9x$

9. Three times a number increased by 9 $3x + 9$

10. The quotient of a number and 4 increased by 2 $\frac{x}{4} + 2$

11. Six times the difference between c and 7 $6(c - 7)$

12. Two times the sum of a number and 11 $2(x + 11)$

CD-104315 • © Carson-Dellosa   81

Name _____ Date _____

Problem Solving

Writing Algebraic Expressions

| Eight more than a number is 28. Find the number. |
| $8 + x = 28$ |
| $8 - 8 + x = 28 - 8$ |
| $x = 20$ |

Write an equation for each expression and solve.

1. The cost of 1 saddle is $220.00. What is the cost of 7 saddles?

    $(\$220)(7) = \$1,540$

2. One-third of a number is ⁻15. Find the number.

    $\frac{x}{3} = ^-15,\ x = ^-45$

3. The cost of 6 cakes is $48.00. What is the cost of each cake?

    $6x = 48,\ x = 8$

4. Four times a number is 52. Find the number.

    $4x = 52,\ x = 13$

5. The product of ⁻9 and a number is 36. Find the number.

    $^-9x = 36,\ x = ^-4$

6. Three times a number is 24. Find the number.

    $3x = 24,\ x = 8$

7. A number increased by 8 is ⁻24. Find the number.

    $x + 8 = ^-24,\ x = ^-32$

82   CD-104315 • © Carson-Dellosa

Name _____ Date _____

Problem Solving

Writing Algebraic Expressions

| A number decreased by 7 is 10. Find the number. |
| $x - 7 = 10$ |
| $x - 7 + 7 = 10 + 7$ |
| $x = 17$ |

Write an equation for each expression and solve.

1. Three times a number is 63. Find the number.

    $3x = 63,\ x = 21$

2. The product of ⁻4 and a number is 28. Find the number.

    $^-4x = 28,\ x = ^-7$

3. One-fourth of a number is 13. Find the number.

    $\frac{x}{4} = 13,\ x = 52$

4. Four times a number is 24. Find the number.

    $4x = 24,\ x = 6$

5. The cost of 6 boxes of cookies is $30.00. What is the cost of each box?

    $6x = \$30.00,\ x = \$5.00$

6. The cost of a television is $234.00. What is the cost of 3 televisions?

    $(\$234)(3) = \$702$

7. A number increased by 10 is 54. Find the number.

    $x + 10 = 54,\ x = 44$

CD-104315 • © Carson-Dellosa   83

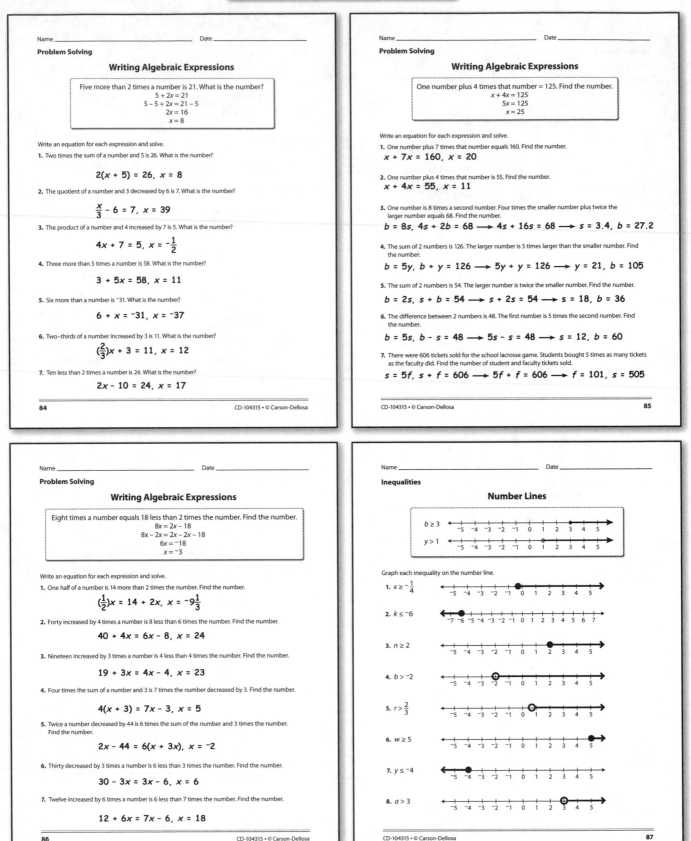

Name _____ Date _____

Problem Solving

Writing Algebraic Expressions

> Five more than 2 times a number is 21. What is the number?
> $5 + 2x = 21$
> $5 - 5 + 2x = 21 - 5$
> $2x = 16$
> $x = 8$

Write an equation for each expression and solve.

1. Two times the sum of a number and 5 is 26. What is the number?

$$2(x + 5) = 26, \ x = 8$$

2. The quotient of a number and 3 decreased by 6 is 7. What is the number?

$$\frac{x}{3} - 6 = 7, \ x = 39$$

3. The product of a number and 4 increased by 7 is 5. What is the number?

$$4x + 7 = 5, \ x = -\frac{1}{2}$$

4. Three more than 5 times a number is 58. What is the number?

$$3 + 5x = 58, \ x = 11$$

5. Six more than a number is ‾31. What is the number?

$$6 + x = {}^-31, \ x = {}^-37$$

6. Two–thirds of a number increased by 3 is 11. What is the number?

$$\left(\frac{2}{3}\right)x + 3 = 11, \ x = 12$$

7. Ten less than 2 times a number is 24. What is the number?

$$2x - 10 = 24, \ x = 17$$

84   CD-104315 • © Carson-Dellosa

Name _____ Date _____

Problem Solving

Writing Algebraic Expressions

> One number plus 4 times that number = 125. Find the number.
> $x + 4x = 125$
> $5x = 125$
> $x = 25$

Write an equation for each expression and solve.

1. One number plus 7 times that number equals 160. Find the number.

$$x + 7x = 160, \ x = 20$$

2. One number plus 4 times that number is 55. Find the number.

$$x + 4x = 55, \ x = 11$$

3. One number is 8 times a second number. Four times the smaller number plus twice the larger number equals 68. Find the number.

$$b = 8s, \ 4s + 2b = 68 \longrightarrow 4s + 16s = 68 \longrightarrow s = 3.4, \ b = 27.2$$

4. The sum of 2 numbers is 126. The larger number is 5 times larger than the smaller number. Find the number.

$$b = 5y, \ b + y = 126 \longrightarrow 5y + y = 126 \longrightarrow y = 21, \ b = 105$$

5. The sum of 2 numbers is 54. The larger number is twice the smaller number. Find the number.

$$b = 2s, \ s + b = 54 \longrightarrow s + 2s = 54 \longrightarrow s = 18, \ b = 36$$

6. The difference between 2 numbers is 48. The first number is 5 times the second number. Find the number.

$$b = 5s, \ b - s = 48 \longrightarrow 5s - s = 48 \longrightarrow s = 12, \ b = 60$$

7. There were 606 tickets sold for the school lacrosse game. Students bought 5 times as many tickets as the faculty did. Find the number of student and faculty tickets sold.

$$s = 5f, \ s + f = 606 \longrightarrow 5f + f = 606 \longrightarrow f = 101, \ s = 505$$

CD-104315 • © Carson-Dellosa   85

Name _____ Date _____

Problem Solving

Writing Algebraic Expressions

> Eight times a number equals 18 less than 2 times the number. Find the number.
> $8x = 2x - 18$
> $8x - 2x = 2x - 2x - 18$
> $6x = {}^-18$
> $x = {}^-3$

Write an equation for each expression and solve.

1. One half of a number is 14 more than 2 times the number. Find the number.

$$\left(\frac{1}{2}\right)x = 14 + 2x, \ x = {}^-9\frac{1}{3}$$

2. Forty increased by 4 times a number is 8 less than 6 times the number. Find the number.

$$40 + 4x = 6x - 8, \ x = 24$$

3. Nineteen increased by 3 times a number is 4 less than 4 times the number. Find the number.

$$19 + 3x = 4x - 4, \ x = 23$$

4. Four times the sum of a number and 3 is 7 times the number decreased by 3. Find the number.

$$4(x + 3) = 7x - 3, \ x = 5$$

5. Twice a number decreased by 44 is 6 times the sum of the number and 3 times the number. Find the number.

$$2x - 44 = 6(x + 3x), \ x = {}^-2$$

6. Thirty decreased by 3 times a number is 6 less than 3 times the number. Find the number.

$$30 - 3x = 3x - 6, \ x = 6$$

7. Twelve increased by 6 times a number is 6 less than 7 times the number. Find the number.

$$12 + 6x = 7x - 6, \ x = 18$$

86   CD-104315 • © Carson-Dellosa

Name _____ Date _____

Inequalities

Number Lines

> $b \geq 3$
> $y > 1$

Graph each inequality on the number line.

1. $x \geq -\frac{1}{4}$

2. $k \leq {}^-6$

3. $n \geq 2$

4. $b > {}^-2$

5. $r > \frac{2}{3}$

6. $w \geq 5$

7. $y \leq {}^-4$

8. $a > 3$

CD-104315 • © Carson-Dellosa   87

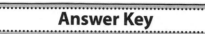

Name _____ Date _____

Inequalities

Solving Inequalities with Addition and Subtraction

$$x + 6 < 4$$
$$x + 6 - 6 < 4 - 6$$
$$x < ^-2$$

Solve each inequality and graph the answer on the number line.

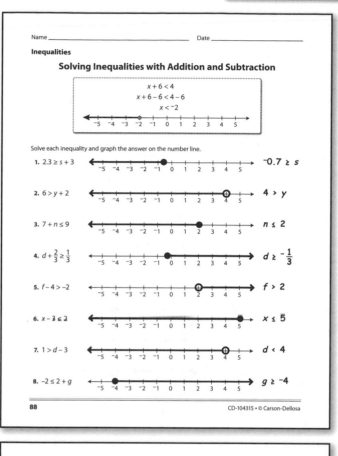

1. $2.3 \geq s + 3$ $^-0.7 \geq s$

2. $6 > y + 2$ $4 > y$

3. $7 + n \leq 9$ $n \leq 2$

4. $d + \frac{2}{3} \geq \frac{1}{3}$ $d \geq ^-\frac{1}{3}$

5. $f - 4 > ^-2$ $f > 2$

6. $x - 3 \leq 2$ $x \leq 5$

7. $1 > d - 3$ $d < 4$

8. $^-2 \leq 2 + g$ $g \geq ^-4$

88   CD-104315 • © Carson-Dellosa

Name _____ Date _____

Inequalities

Solving Inequalities with Multiplication and Division

$$(^-\tfrac{1}{2})x \geq 2$$
$$^-\tfrac{2}{1} \cdot (^-\tfrac{1}{2})x \geq 2(^-\tfrac{2}{1})$$
$$x \leq ^-4$$

Always change the sign when multiplying or dividing by a negative number.

Solve each inequality and graph the answer on the number line.

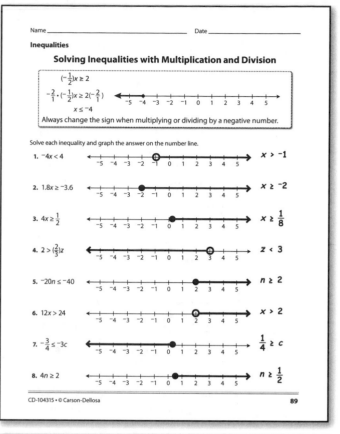

1. $^-4x < 4$ $x > ^-1$

2. $1.8x \geq ^-3.6$ $x \geq ^-2$

3. $4x \geq \frac{1}{2}$ $x \geq \frac{1}{8}$

4. $2 > (\frac{2}{3})z$ $z < 3$

5. $^-20n \leq ^-40$ $n \geq 2$

6. $12x > 24$ $x > 2$

7. $^-\frac{3}{4} \leq ^-3c$ $\frac{1}{4} \geq c$

8. $4n \geq 2$ $n \geq \frac{1}{2}$

CD-104315 • © Carson-Dellosa   89

Name _____ Date _____

Inequalities

Solving Inequalities

Solve each inequality and graph the answer on the number line.

1. $r \geq 3$ $r \geq 3$

2. $x > ^-2$ $x > ^-2$

3. $^-r \leq 1$ $r \geq ^-1$

4. $x \geq 3$ $x \geq 3$

5. $t \leq ^-4$ $t \leq ^-4$

6. $2c \geq 2$ $c \geq 1$

7. $^-4 \geq 2b$ $b \leq ^-2$

8. $m \geq ^-4$ $m \geq ^-4$

9. $e + 1 \leq 3$ $e \leq 2$

10. $5t \geq ^-5$ $t \geq ^-1$

90   CD-104315 • © Carson-Dellosa

Name _____ Date _____

Inequalities

Solving Inequalities

Solve each inequality and graph the answer on the number line.

1. $c + 1 > ^-4$ $c > ^-5$

2. $6.5c < 6.5$ $c < 1$

3. $^-4 \geq s - (^-2)$ $s \leq ^-6$

4. $(\frac{1}{2})y > ^-5$ $y > ^-10$

5. $d - 4.5 \geq ^-1.5$ $d \geq 3$

6. $^-14.5 \leq x + ^-21.5$ $x \geq 7$

7. $^-13 < g - 12$ $g > ^-1$

8. $h + 9 > 12$ $h > 3$

9. $^-\frac{n}{3} \geq 2$ $n \leq ^-6$

10. $10 > r + 14$ $r < ^-4$

CD-104315 • © Carson-Dellosa   91

Name _____ Date _____

Inequalities

Solving Inequalities

$$-20x + 8 > 4x - 40$$
$$-20x + 20x + 8 > 4x + 20x - 40$$
$$8 > 24x - 40$$
$$48 > 24x$$
$$2 > x$$

Solve each inequality and graph the answer on the number line.

1. $-6\frac{1}{3} \geq k + \frac{2}{3}$ $k \leq {}^-7$

2. $h - 3 \leq 2$ $h \leq 5$

3. $a - 2.07 \geq 3.93$ $a \geq 6$

4. $1.3q \geq 8.7$ $q \geq 6.69$

5. $-11 < k + {}^-13$ $k > 2$

6. $-14 \geq h - 8$ $h \leq {}^-6$

7. $13 > 12m + 7$ $m < \frac{1}{2}$

8. $(\frac{2}{5})b \geq {}^-2$ $b \geq {}^-5$

9. $-\frac{r}{2} \leq 5$ $r \geq {}^-10$

10. $-14t > 56$ $t < {}^-4$

Name _____ Date _____

Inequalities

Solving Inequalities

Solve each inequality and graph the answer on the number line.

1. $-14n > 98$ $n < {}^-7$

2. $2.7d \geq 21.6$ $d \geq 8$

3. $w + 8.4 \geq 5.4$ $w \geq {}^-3$

4. $(\frac{2}{7})d \leq {}^-2$ $d \leq {}^-7$

5. $-3\frac{1}{8} \leq h - \frac{1}{8}$ $h \geq {}^-3$

6. $-13.4 \geq j - 20.4$ $j \leq 7$

7. $7 > 9s + {}^-2$ $s < 1$

8. $-12m < m - 26$ $m > 2$

9. $-\frac{t}{2} \leq 2$ $t \geq {}^-4$

10. $k + 3\frac{2}{5} \geq {}^-1\frac{3}{5}$ $k \geq {}^-5$

Name _____ Date _____

Inequalities

Solving Inequalities with Multiple Operations

$$-12x + 3 \geq 51$$
$$-12x + 3 - 3 \geq 51 - 3$$
$$-12x \geq 48$$
$$x \leq {}^-4$$

Solve each inequality and graph the answer on the number line.

1. $-5 > 4x - 7$ $x < \frac{1}{2}$

2. $3(2c - 2) \geq 48$ $c \geq 9$

3. $-15 > {}^-4x - 75$ $x > {}^-15$

4. $-4(4x + 4) \geq 32$ $x \leq {}^-3$

5. $5x - 9 > 21$ $x > 6$

6. $-2x - 10 \geq 6$ $x \leq {}^-8$

7. $20 < {}^-12.8 + 8x$ $x > 4.1$

8. $-6(3t + 3) \leq 18$ $t \geq {}^-2$

Name _____ Date _____

Inequalities

Solving Inequalities with Variables on Both Sides

$$-20x + 10 < 5x - 15$$
$$-20x + 20x + 10 < 5x + 20x - 15$$
$$10 + 15 < 25x - 15 + 15$$
$$25 < 25x$$
$$1 < x$$

Solve each inequality and graph the answer on the number line.

1. $23 - 12x > {}^-(7 + 2x)$ $x < 3$

2. $3(2x - 4) > 4x + 4$ $x > 8$

3. $3(s - 4) \geq 6s + 12$ $s \leq {}^-8$

4. $4c + 6 < (3 + 2c)$ $c < {}^-1\frac{1}{2}$

5. $8 - e > 3e + 12$ $e < {}^-1$

6. $-3(5t - 12) \leq 4t - 21$ $t \geq 3$

7. $5c + 1 > 3(3 + c)$ $c > 4$

8. $x - 4x \geq {}^-5x - 10$ $x \geq {}^-5$

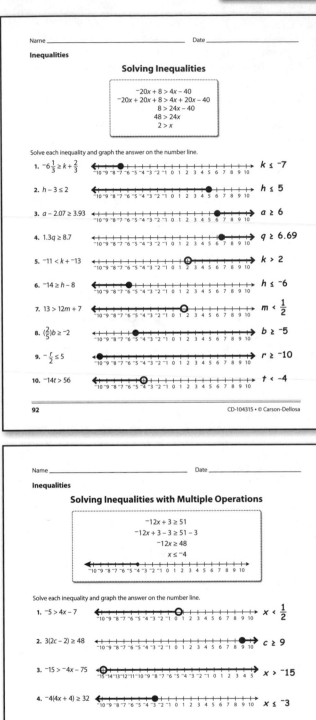

Page 96

Name _____ Date _____

Inequalities

Practice Solving Inequalities

Solve each inequality and graph the answer on the number line.

1. $-4 \geq h + 1$ ⟵—————●———————⟶ $h \leq -5$
   $-10\ -9\ -8\ -7\ -6\ -5\ -4\ -3\ -2\ -1\ 0\ 1\ 2\ 3\ 4\ 5\ 6\ 7\ 8\ 9\ 10$

2. $2.8h \leq 8.4$ ⟵————————————●———⟶ $h \leq 3$
   $-10\ -9\ -8\ -7\ -6\ -5\ -4\ -3\ -2\ -1\ 0\ 1\ 2\ 3\ 4\ 5\ 6\ 7\ 8\ 9\ 10$

3. $r + 3 \leq 5$ ⟵———————————●————⟶ $r \leq 2$
   $-10\ -9\ -8\ -7\ -6\ -5\ -4\ -3\ -2\ -1\ 0\ 1\ 2\ 3\ 4\ 5\ 6\ 7\ 8\ 9\ 10$

4. $2 \geq 2x - 8$ ⟵———————————————●——⟶ $x \leq 5$
   $-10\ -9\ -8\ -7\ -6\ -5\ -4\ -3\ -2\ -1\ 0\ 1\ 2\ 3\ 4\ 5\ 6\ 7\ 8\ 9\ 10$

5. $(\frac{2}{3})k \geq -6$ ⟵—●————————————————⟶ $k \geq -9$
   $-10\ -9\ -8\ -7\ -6\ -5\ -4\ -3\ -2\ -1\ 0\ 1\ 2\ 3\ 4\ 5\ 6\ 7\ 8\ 9\ 10$

6. $-13t > 78$ ⟵——○———————————————⟶ $t < -6$
   $-10\ -9\ -8\ -7\ -6\ -5\ -4\ -3\ -2\ -1\ 0\ 1\ 2\ 3\ 4\ 5\ 6\ 7\ 8\ 9\ 10$

7. $9 \leq 6y - 15$ ⟵——————————————●———⟶ $y \geq 4$
   $-10\ -9\ -8\ -7\ -6\ -5\ -4\ -3\ -2\ -1\ 0\ 1\ 2\ 3\ 4\ 5\ 6\ 7\ 8\ 9\ 10$

8. $32.7 \geq t + 25.7$ ⟵—————————————————●—⟶ $t \leq 7$
   $-10\ -9\ -8\ -7\ -6\ -5\ -4\ -3\ -2\ -1\ 0\ 1\ 2\ 3\ 4\ 5\ 6\ 7\ 8\ 9\ 10$

9. $-7e \geq 21$ ⟵————————●—————————⟶ $e \leq -3$
   $-10\ -9\ -8\ -7\ -6\ -5\ -4\ -3\ -2\ -1\ 0\ 1\ 2\ 3\ 4\ 5\ 6\ 7\ 8\ 9\ 10$

10. $12d < d + 11$ ⟵————————————○—————⟶ $d < 1$
    $-10\ -9\ -8\ -7\ -6\ -5\ -4\ -3\ -2\ -1\ 0\ 1\ 2\ 3\ 4\ 5\ 6\ 7\ 8\ 9\ 10$

CD-104315 • © Carson-Dellosa

Page 97

Name _____ Date _____

Inequalities

Practice Solving Inequalities

Solve each inequality and graph the answer on the number line.

1. $8c - 7 + c < 13 + 5c$ ⟵————————————————○——⟶ $c < 5$
   $-10\ -9\ -8\ -7\ -6\ -5\ -4\ -3\ -2\ -1\ 0\ 1\ 2\ 3\ 4\ 5\ 6\ 7\ 8\ 9\ 10$

2. $5(3w - 4) < 8w + 8$ ⟵———————————————○———⟶ $w < 4$
   $-10\ -9\ -8\ -7\ -6\ -5\ -4\ -3\ -2\ -1\ 0\ 1\ 2\ 3\ 4\ 5\ 6\ 7\ 8\ 9\ 10$

3. $3(4c + 3) + 1 \leq 2(c - 5)$ ⟵———————●————————⟶ $c \leq -2$
   $-10\ -9\ -8\ -7\ -6\ -5\ -4\ -3\ -2\ -1\ 0\ 1\ 2\ 3\ 4\ 5\ 6\ 7\ 8\ 9\ 10$

4. $12(m - 1) \leq 5(m + 3) - 6$ ⟵————————————●———⟶ $m \leq 3$
   $-10\ -9\ -8\ -7\ -6\ -5\ -4\ -3\ -2\ -1\ 0\ 1\ 2\ 3\ 4\ 5\ 6\ 7\ 8\ 9\ 10$

5. $\frac{1}{2} < (\frac{1}{2})x - 2$ ⟵————————————————○——⟶ $x > 5$
   $-10\ -9\ -8\ -7\ -6\ -5\ -4\ -3\ -2\ -1\ 0\ 1\ 2\ 3\ 4\ 5\ 6\ 7\ 8\ 9\ 10$

6. $4x + 7 < x - 8$ ⟵—————○—————————————⟶ $x < -5$
   $-10\ -9\ -8\ -7\ -6\ -5\ -4\ -3\ -2\ -1\ 0\ 1\ 2\ 3\ 4\ 5\ 6\ 7\ 8\ 9\ 10$

7. $2(3a + 4) \geq 3a - 4$ ⟵——————●———————————⟶ $a \geq -4$
   $-10\ -9\ -8\ -7\ -6\ -5\ -4\ -3\ -2\ -1\ 0\ 1\ 2\ 3\ 4\ 5\ 6\ 7\ 8\ 9\ 10$

8. $48 > x + 50$ ⟵————————○—————————⟶ $x < -2$
   $-10\ -9\ -8\ -7\ -6\ -5\ -4\ -3\ -2\ -1\ 0\ 1\ 2\ 3\ 4\ 5\ 6\ 7\ 8\ 9\ 10$

9. $-5(4a + 4) \geq 40$ ⟵————————●—————————⟶ $a \leq -3$
   $-10\ -9\ -8\ -7\ -6\ -5\ -4\ -3\ -2\ -1\ 0\ 1\ 2\ 3\ 4\ 5\ 6\ 7\ 8\ 9\ 10$

10. $11x \geq -44$ ⟵——————●————————————⟶ $x \geq -4$
    $-10\ -9\ -8\ -7\ -6\ -5\ -4\ -3\ -2\ -1\ 0\ 1\ 2\ 3\ 4\ 5\ 6\ 7\ 8\ 9\ 10$

CD-104315 • © Carson-Dellosa

Page 98

Name _____ Date _____

Ordered Pairs and Graphing

Plotting Points

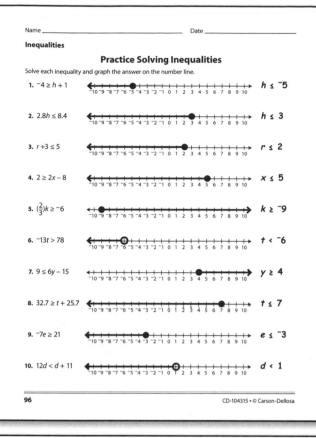

$(x,y) = (2, -3)$ Over 2 to the right and down 3
$(x,y) = (-4, 1)$ Over 4 to the left and up 1
$(x,y) = (1, 3)$ Over 1 to the right and up 3

Plot and label the following points on the graph.

A(3, -4)
B(6, 2)
C(0, -2)
D(1, 7)
E(3, -3)
F(2, -6)
G(-3, 4)
H(-1, -4)
I(3, 0)
J(2, 5)

CD-104315 • © Carson-Dellosa

Page 99

Name _____ Date _____

Ordered Pairs and Graphing

Plotting Points

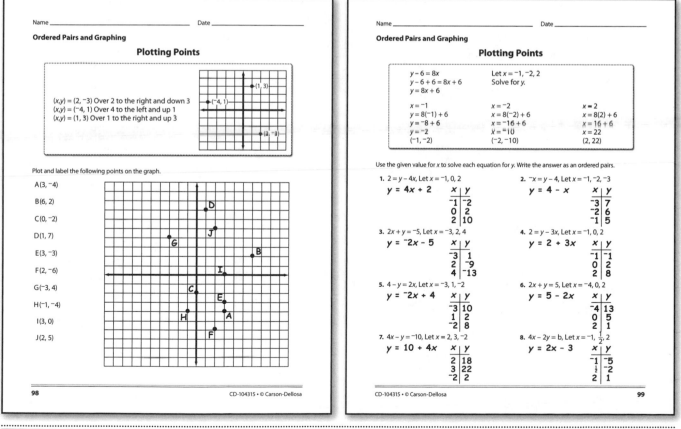

$y - 6 = 8x$	Let $x = -1, -2, 2$	
$y - 6 + 6 = 8x + 6$	Solve for y.	
$y = 8x + 6$		
$x = -1$	$x = -2$	$x = 2$
$y = 8(-1) + 6$	$x = 8(-2) + 6$	$x = 8(2) + 6$
$y = -8 + 6$	$x = -16 + 6$	$x = 16 + 6$
$y = -2$	$x = -10$	$x = 22$
$(-1, -2)$	$(-2, -10)$	$(2, 22)$

Use the given value for x to solve each equation for y. Write the answer as an ordered pairs.

1. $2 = y - 4x$, Let $x = -1, 0, 2$
   $y = 4x + 2$

x	y
-1	-2
0	2
2	10

2. $-x = y - 4$, Let $x = -1, -2, -3$
   $y = 4 - x$

x	y
-3	7
-2	6
-1	5

3. $2x + y = -5$, Let $x = -3, 2, 4$
   $y = -2x - 5$

x	y
-3	1
2	-9
4	-13

4. $2 = y - 3x$, Let $x = -1, 0, 2$
   $y = 2 + 3x$

x	y
-1	-1
0	2
2	8

5. $4 - y = 2x$, Let $x = -3, 1, -2$
   $y = -2x + 4$

x	y
-3	10
1	2
-2	8

6. $2x + y = 5$, Let $x = -4, 0, 2$
   $y = 5 - 2x$

x	y
-4	13
0	5
2	1

7. $4x - y = -10$, Let $x = 2, 3, -2$
   $y = 10 + 4x$

x	y
2	18
3	22
-2	2

8. $4x - 2y = b$, Let $x = -1, \frac{1}{2}, 2$
   $y = 2x - 3$

x	y
-1	-5
$\frac{1}{2}$	-2
2	1

CD-104315 • © Carson-Dellosa

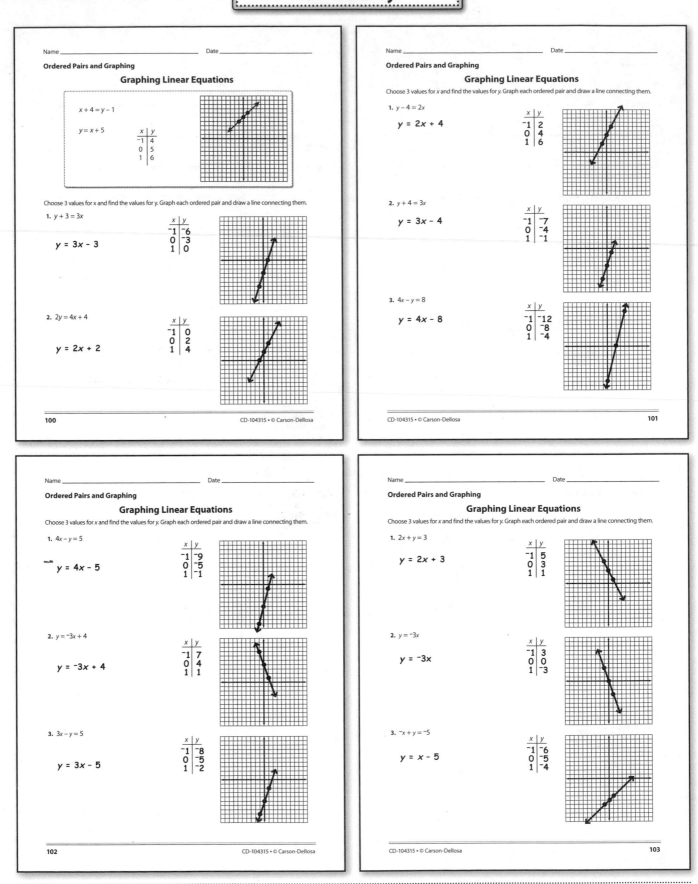

Name _____ Date _____

Ordered Pairs and Graphing

Graphing Linear Equations

$x + 4 = y - 1$

$y = x + 5$

x	y
-1	4
0	5
1	6

Choose 3 values for x and find the values for y. Graph each ordered pair and draw a line connecting them.

1. $y + 3 = 3x$

$y = 3x - 3$

x	y
-1	-6
0	-3
1	0

2. $2y = 4x + 4$

$y = 2x + 2$

x	y
-1	0
0	2
1	4

100   CD-104315 • © Carson-Dellosa

Name _____ Date _____

Ordered Pairs and Graphing

Graphing Linear Equations

Choose 3 values for x and find the values for y. Graph each ordered pair and draw a line connecting them.

1. $y - 4 = 2x$

$y = 2x + 4$

x	y
-1	2
0	4
1	6

2. $y + 4 = 3x$

$y = 3x - 4$

x	y
-1	-7
0	-4
1	-1

3. $4x - y = 8$

$y = 4x - 8$

x	y
-1	-12
0	-8
1	-4

CD-104315 • © Carson-Dellosa   101

Name _____ Date _____

Ordered Pairs and Graphing

Graphing Linear Equations

Choose 3 values for x and find the values for y. Graph each ordered pair and draw a line connecting them.

1. $4x - y = 5$

$y = 4x - 5$

x	y
-1	-9
0	-5
1	-1

2. $y = -3x + 4$

$y = -3x + 4$

x	y
-1	7
0	4
1	1

3. $3x - y = 5$

$y = 3x - 5$

x	y
-1	-8
0	-5
1	-2

102   CD-104315 • © Carson-Dellosa

Name _____ Date _____

Ordered Pairs and Graphing

Graphing Linear Equations

Choose 3 values for x and find the values for y. Graph each ordered pair and draw a line connecting them.

1. $2x + y = 3$

$y = 2x + 3$

x	y
-1	5
0	3
1	1

2. $y = -3x$

$y = -3x$

x	y
-1	3
0	0
1	-3

3. $-x + y = -5$

$y = x - 5$

x	y
-1	-6
0	-5
1	-4

CD-104315 • © Carson-Dellosa   103

Congratulations!

_____

receives this award for

_____

Signed _____

Date _____

Write as a decimal. $\dfrac{2}{3}$ © CD	Write as a decimal. $\dfrac{1}{12}$ © CD	Write as a decimal. $\dfrac{1}{5}$ © CD	Write as a decimal. $\dfrac{1}{4}$ © CD
Write as a decimal. $\dfrac{3}{10}$ © CD	Write as a decimal. $\dfrac{33}{100}$ © CD	Write as a decimal. $\dfrac{23}{40}$ © CD	Write as a decimal. $\dfrac{7}{1000}$ © CD
Write as a fraction. 0.45 © CD	Write as a fraction. 0.005 © CD	Write as a fraction. 0.25 © CD	Write as a fraction. 0.15 © CD
Write as a fraction. 0.05 © CD	Write as a fraction. 0.2 © CD	Write as a fraction. 0.125 © CD	Write as a fraction. 0.7 © CD

0.25	0.2	$0.08\overline{3}$	$0.\overline{6}$
0.007	0.575	0.33	0.3
$\dfrac{3}{20}$	$\dfrac{1}{4}$	$\dfrac{1}{200}$	$\dfrac{9}{20}$
$\dfrac{7}{10}$	$\dfrac{1}{8}$	$\dfrac{1}{5}$	$\dfrac{1}{20}$

Round to the nearest whole number.	Round to the nearest whole number.	Round to the nearest whole number.
45.21	356.4	901.14
© CD	© CD	© CD

Round to the nearest ten.	Round to the nearest hundred.	Round to the nearest hundred.
341.5	3,357	42,555.6
© CD	© CD	© CD

Round to the nearest tenth.	Round to the nearest tenth.	Round to the nearest tenth.
32.54	201.15	2,343.38	4.23
© CD	© CD	© CD

Round to the nearest hundredth.	Round to the nearest hundredth.	Round to the nearest hundredth.
5.455	3,295.675	203.421	12.901
© CD	© CD	© CD

901   4,515   356   45

42,600   304,300   3,360   340

4.2   2,343.4   201.2   32.5

12.90   203.42   3,295.68   5.46

$-36 \div 9$

$4 \times (-5)$

$-15 \div 5$

$(5)(-12)$

$49 \div (-7)$

$-44 \div (-11)$

$24 \div (-6)$

$-36 \div (-12)$

$-4 \times (-2)$

$-63 \div (-6)$

$(-7)(5)$

$(-11)(10)$

$(-7)(-2)$

$(-4) \cdot (4)$

$56 \div (-8)$

$-12 \cdot 6$

−4	−7	8	14
−20	4	10.5	−16
−3	−4	−35	−7
−60	3	−110	−72

$3(5 + 4) =$

$6 - 49 \div 7 =$

$21 \div (2 + 5) =$

$81 \div 3^2 - 2 =$

$11 - 3 + 5 =$

$3 \cdot 5 - 4 \cdot 8 =$

$7 + 2 \cdot 2 =$

$15 \div 5 \times 2 =$

$14 \div 2 \times 6 =$

$8 + 6 \div 3 =$

$35 \div 5 + 3 =$

$(4 + 1)^2 =$

$5 + 3 \times 4 =$

$24 \div 6 - 2 =$

$5 + 3(20 \div 4) =$

$3^2 - 2 \cdot 3 =$

27	13	42	17
−1	−17	10	2
3	11	10	20
7	6	25	3

$3 - 7 =$

$-5 + (-5) =$

$16 - 8 =$

$4 - (-3) =$

$-3 - 5 =$

$7 + (-6) =$

$4 - 8 =$

$-5 + 8 =$

$-12 + 8 =$

$-5 + (-9) =$

$-19 - (-4) =$

$-2 + (-6) =$

$-8 + 14 =$

$-4 - (-2) =$

$15 + (-7) =$

$-13 + 7 =$

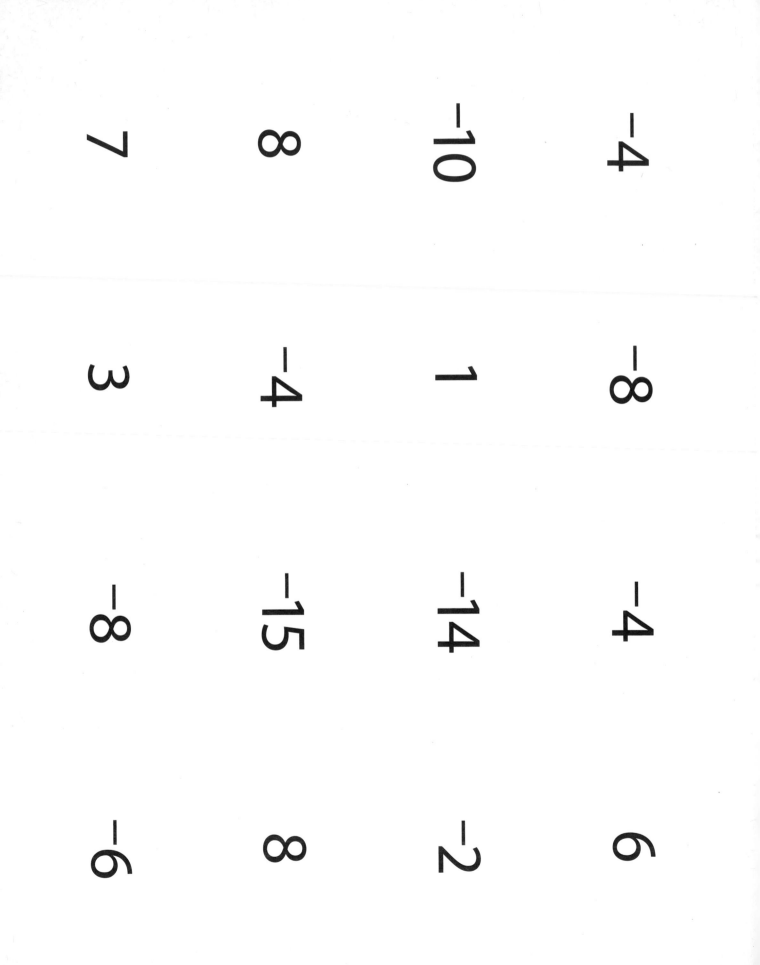

$2 + 6 =$

$(-6) - (-6) =$

$2 - 9 =$

$(-3) - 5 =$

$-11 - (-5) =$

$7 - (-3) =$

$5 - 10 =$

$-12 - (-4) =$

$3 - 5 =$

$-4 + (-3) =$

$-3 - 3 =$

$-4 + 5 =$

$-3 - (-4) =$

$-4 - (-8) =$

$7 - 13 =$

$7 - (-4) =$

8	-6	-2	1
0	10	-7	4
-7	-5	-6	-6
-8	-8	1	11